End

MW00805567

There is a powerful healing that comes when control is replaced with surrender. Mimi's story is a doorway that ushers in the life-giving grace and truth of Jesus. I know that in the pages of this book, many will find hope, strength, and inspiration for their own journey, just as I have.

— **Matthew Hein**, recording artist with I AM THEY

Mimi Kroger's book *Holy Spirit, Help Me Heal* takes you on a journey to discovering the kindness of the Holy Spirit. With raw open-heartedness, Mimi shares her story of healing and provides opportunity for people to reflect and engage with the Holy Spirit in a practical way at each step along the journey. This story of redemption and healing will captivate and inspire you to trust the One who is altogether faithful and trustworthy.

— **Katherine Ruonala**, senior leader at Glory City Church, author of *Living in the Miraculous, Double for Your Trouble, Wilderness to Wonders, Life with the Holy Spirit* and *Speak Life* www.katherineruonala.com

Mimi's book *Holy Spirit, Help Me Heal* is a guide on how to draw closer to Jesus and on how to heal in body, soul, and spirit. He's our hope for healing, and through her writing, she shares the truth about who God is for us. She talks about her own battles, and you can feel her heart for the Lord coming through her words, bringing hope to anyone who reads it. Let this book draw you closer to God. Be sure to check out her powerful bonus chapter, "Beauty for Ashes: Even if You Start the Fire."

— **Francie & Duane Chapman**, Dog the Bounty Hunter

If you are searching for healing of the spirit and body, *Holy Spirit, Help Me Heal* is a compelling read to help you start along the path to healing, to strengthen your faith, and to renew your body through the Holy Spirit. Although Mimi describes her medical journey, she focuses on her healing through the Holy Spirit—not just physical healing, but the complete emotional and spiritual healing that comes from knowing you have worth and are unconditionally loved by God. God is unfailing in His love and unchanging in His desire to heal us through the Spirit. Take this journey with Mimi—read, reflect, and worship in order to guide your own restoration.

— **Heather A. Shull, MD**, care team medical director

What an honor for our first single to be used as a "Heart Connection" in Mimi's book. Her journey to a healthy and balanced life dependent on the Holy Spirit is more than inspiring, it is *LIFE-GIVING*!

— **CAIN**, song "Rise Up (Lazarus)"

Mimi's story reveals the heart of God for each one of us. Through her beautiful words, Mimi shows how to grab hold of God's goodness and never let go! Let the healing begin as you open up this powerful book.

— **Amy Elaine Martinez**, host of the *Past to Power Podcast* and author of *Becoming a Victory Girl* www.amyelaine.com

A powerful personal account of leaning on the Holy Spirit for healing of the body, soul, and spirit. Mimi's stories are inspiring and vulnerable. There's nothing like hope to transform your health and your life.

— **Jendayi Harris**, author of *The Chubby Church* www.thechubbychurch.com

We could fill a page with descriptors of Mimi Kroger—faithful, fun, and vivacious, to name a few. However, the word triumphant just might top our list.

Holy Spirit, Help Me Heal is a story beautifully told of a tremendous battle, literally a battle of life and death. Mimi Kroger faced terrific challenges, including lupus and a kidney transplant. With vulnerability and great grace, she tells of her battle. But more importantly, she tells of her love affair with Jesus. Intimacy with the precious Holy Spirit and the Word of God, coupled with strong faith, have healed her mind, body, and spirit.

Whether your battle is physical or emotional or if it involves deep soul wounds, this book will lead you on a journey towards health and wholeness. Find your "Jesus chair," your quiet place for soul searching, scripture contemplation and dialogue with Holy Spirit. As you engage with these pages and the Lord, let Mimi's story and wisdom help usher you into the astonishing wellness of abundant life.

And the bonus chapter!! Trust us; you will really want to get Mimi's "Beauty for Ashes: Even if You Start the Fire." We loved how she told more of her amazing testimony. If you are searching for the meaning of grace—crazy, extravagant grace—this bonus chapter is for you.

As Mimi penned, "It's time for the real you to shine!"

– **Dr. Dan & Linda Wilson**, authors of 5 books including *Seven Secrets of a Supernatural Marriage*
www.supernaturalmarriage.org

Mimi gives the valuable message of God's perfect love in her book, *Holy Spirit, Help Me Heal*. She reveals His true nature through the words she writes. As she shares vulnerable experiences from her life, you will receive help and hope.

– **Pastor J.R. Polhemus**, Castle Rock, Colorado

Holy Spirit, Help Me Heal kept me turning pages as I journeyed with Mimi down the path of near-death and back to wholeness again. Her perseverance toward purpose, passion to help others, and plan to partner with the Holy Spirit teaches us to have a life of abundance. In her ongoing conversation with the Holy Spirit, Mimi is living proof of God's glorious inheritance. Be prepared to be changed as you are immersed in the greatest love of all.

> **– Angela Dee Smith**, speaker, teacher, and artist, author of *Voiceless, Spencer's Story* www.angeladee.life

With grace and humility, this book is meant to help heal the broken heart, mind, and body. Mimi brilliantly and passionately brings the reader into every scene leaving you with hope that you too can push through whatever is gripping you or in the past has gripped you to the core.

> **– Moe & Paige Becnel**, founders of Blending A Family Ministry and authors of several books including the best-selling *God Breathes on Blended Families* www.blendingafamily.com

Mimi Kroger explores the depths of physical, spiritual, and emotional healing by encountering God's kindness and restoration. This book seamlessly takes you through her journey of wholeness, God's kindness, and God's ultimate goal of bringing each of us into His family and becoming more than conquerors through Christ Jesus. I recommend this book as a guide to help you along your journey.

> **– Brian Fenimore**, founder of Plumbline Ministries www.plumblinem.com

Holy Spirit, Help Me Heal

Holy Spirit, Help Me Heal

Overcoming Disease & Dysfunction through Spirit Connection & Soul Healing

MIMI KROGER

Dedication

To My Loving Father God,
Saving Friend Jesus,
and
to My Guide and Comfort,
the Holy Spirit,
Thank You for Healing Me.

Disclaimer

The ideas and information presented in this book are based on the author's opinion and personal experience and are not intended to be used, nor should they be used, to diagnose, treat, cure, or prevent any medical condition or disease, including but not limited to, physical or psychological issues. For the diagnosis or treatment of any medical condition, consult a licensed professional.

The author is not a healthcare provider and intends, along with the publisher, that none of the information within this book be considered professional, psychological, nutritional, or medical advice. Please consult with your physician or healthcare specialist regarding any material in this book you intend to implement. Before you begin any self-improvement changes, consult your physician or other healthcare practitioner to ensure that any information utilized from this book will not harm you. Statements made within this book have not been evaluated by the U.S. Food and Drug Administration or any licensed medical or health-care professional.

The author and publisher of this book are not held liable or responsible, to any person or entity or third parties, for action taken, application, or results achieved or consequences, directly or indirectly, from the use or implementation of any content provided, including any information contained in works that were referenced or cited. Author and publisher do not endorse any websites or sources mentioned. All references are listed for informational purposes only with the understanding that websites may change. While best efforts have been taken in the preparation and presentation of this book, the author and publisher disclaim and assume no liability concerning the accuracy or completeness of the contents of this book, including any of the websites or works cited. The author and publisher present this book and its contents on an "as is" basis, making no representations or warranties of any kind that information within this work is accurate, complete, or current.

No guarantees or outcomes are expressed or implied by the author or publisher. Neither the author nor publisher shall be liable for any physical, psychological, emotional, financial, or commercial damages to its reader or any third parties, or alleged to have been caused, directly or indirectly, from information contained within this book; including, but not limited to, special, incidental, consequential, or other damages and claims. Opinions and recommendations contained within this book may not be suitable for your situation. The full responsibility for any choices, actions, and results based on reading or following the information contained within this book is solely upon the reader. Use of this book implies your full release of liability to the author and publisher and complete acceptance of this disclaimer.

A Gift for You

As a special thank you for reading
Holy Spirit, Help Me Heal,
I would be honored to pray for you by name,
and you will also receive a bonus chapter,
"Beauty for Ashes: Even if You Start the Fire."

Receive your free gift at mimikrogerauthor.com.

Contents

Part 3: Prospering in Soul & Body

Introduction

Are There Challenges You Think You Can't Overcome?

There was a yearning inside.

I wanted to pass the class so badly. Adding this knowledge to my twenty-five-plus years of experience in the health and fitness industry would provide the extra edge I was looking for. Including it in my toolbox could further help my clients struggling with weight, eating, health issues, and life in general.

I was already a nationally certified personal trainer and nutrition guide. I knew if I chose to let go of my fears and applied myself to the task ahead, I'd also earn the title of a behavior change specialist.

Now middle-aged, it was eons since I was in a school setting. What was ahead felt so daunting. There was a considerable amount of information I'd be tested on, and I was apprehensive about this new learning environment.

We didn't have online courses in my day. What we did have, were self-decorated manila Pee-Chee folders with built-in calculators, in the form of a times table square, conveniently located on the inner flap.

Back then, I could smell the potent Aqua Net-infused hair that produced the coveted tall and stiff hairdos of my fellow students, even before I entered the classroom.

One day a week when the third-period bell rang, dressed in full armor—that is, in our Z. Cavaricci jeans with folded over and rolled up bottoms, our Esprit bags replete with heavy Trapper Keepers, and our Pee Chee masterpieces—we all dutifully filed into the same room in front of computers the size of microwave ovens. With Dire Straits tunes floating in my head, I felt comfort in knowing we were all in this whole learning thing together.

Forward years later, where I sat, alone with my racing heart, staring sheepishly at my laptop—definitely much smaller in size than the computers of my past, but at this moment, more intimidating.

My mind was flooded with anxious thoughts.

Could I follow this online process that was so foreign to me? Would I do well enough on the exams to get my certificate? Why in the world am I so nervous?

I tried to soothe myself with words from within.

Learning new ways of doing things is scary, but you'll be ok.

Even with that silent affirmation, my inner life insisted on shaking and rattling like the tail of a snake.

That was it!

The same enemy, who came to Eve in the form of a serpent, was attempting to rattle my soul too.

I came against his lies with the bits of wisdom I'd gained from diligently reading my Bible since 1996. Time after time (likely not first coined by Cyndi Lauper, but she wrote a song with the same title nonetheless), the faithful Word of God had proven to be my rescue, even without Scripture reference.

I mean, who has time for chapter and verse when the enemy's arrows are flying venomously and without restraint in an attempt to decimate its target?

Me!

I armed myself for battle, wielding the Word of God like a sword. I quickly and out loud returned his faint hiss with a roar.

"I will not be shaken! Greater is He that is in me; I can do all things through Christ who gives me strength!"

I felt a certain level of power and comfort wash over me as I clicked on the tab that revealed the first of what seemed to be a mountain of modules. I refused the overwhelm that was striving to creep into the recesses of my mind and slither over my heart.

At least the topics are interesting, I told myself.

That thought was followed by other introspections. The primary one being that my heart ached to help those hurting with the same struggles I had once faced. I was motivated but still felt uneasy.

The fear of the unknown held me captive, and the magnitude of lessons ahead taunted me. I knew this different learning process and the amount of work before me would feel less daunting by simply beginning.

One bite at a time is how you eat an elephant, I reasoned. Or *one click at a time*, I should say.

Surely, this was an elephant, but I was equipped from deep within, knowing the Lion of Judah was on my side.

Overcoming chronic illness and the slew of other things that may be connected to its continued grip on your life may also feel daunting, mountainous, and even impossible—especially if you've struggled with it for a long period of time.

Believe me, I'm not comparing debilitating pain and countless missed life events, due to illness, with a behavior change class! I realize the feelings of discouragement and overwhelm are, to a degree, known only by those who have suffered with it year after year.

Overcoming is possible, and I'd like to show you how!

Well, I'm pleased to tell you, I passed the class! A behavior change specialist certificate sits framed on my office wall, with my very own name on it. It's not the most significant thing I've conquered, though.

I overcame systemic lupus, an autoimmune disease.

And if I can do it, so can you!

One bite at a time, it's my honor and privilege to share with you my journey to health and wholeness. My prayer is that you'll find your own insights as you read this book and that you will also come into a place of healing, with the help of the Holy Spirit, who desires to be your Counselor and Guide.

I know, if God did it for me, He will do it for you!

With the last name Kroger, I'm often asked if I'm associated with the lucrative Kroger empire—in my neck of the Colorado woods, one of the local grocery chains parented by the Kroger company is named King Soopers—I always used to reply to that question with an adamant, *"I wish!"*

The truth is, I'm part of the most prestigious family there is, the body of believers! All born-again believers can say they are sons and daughters of the *real* King and the bride of Christ.

Yet, proclaiming and truly knowing something are two different things. Much of this book will delve into how we go from just intellectual knowledge that keeps us in the chains of illness, dysfunction, and the heartache of unfulfilled lives, to Divine revelation brought on by the Holy Spirit; He changes everything!

I also happen to be the bride of someone named Ben Kroger. I never thought I'd marry again, after the pain of divorce, but when he asked for my hand in marriage, as feeble as it was while in the middle of chemo treatments, that said it all.

He's pretty much my dream guy for many reasons, but would you believe he makes the bed every day and does all the laundry? Sure, handling domestic duties makes for a pretty great hubby, but it doesn't compare to being fully loved by a man who's been instrumental in keeping me on this side of Heaven for years.

I'll share more about his pivotal role as well as the participation of many others who became literal lifelines in my journey. First, let me tell you about the most important one.

His name is Nathan, my one and only.

My *why* for pursuing freedom, health, and wholeness

I beam with pride in sharing that my son just completed his third year of college. He likely doesn't realize how essential to my healing process he was—he gave me a reason to survive; that's one of the big things a child does for you.

When the pain of chronic illness strikes, it can steal the desire and fortitude it takes to carry on. To watch him grow into the young man he is now is something I refused to be without, and so a warrior was born.

The fighter within refused the idea that I might not get to see my son have his own children someday. I was determined my future would absolutely involve being called *"Glam-ma."* Even if

Nathan rolls his eyes when I insist that name is more suitable than Grandma when the time comes.

My goal is to be the kind of glam-ma that's able to partner in a game of hopscotch and insist on gliding down slippery slides, with hair blowing in the breeze, right alongside my son's own children.

That meant sickness and everything connected to its grip on my life had to go.

When thrust into the pit of chronic illness, the hunger of a momma bear with a growing cub finds the fervor to mount up and dig through whatever trenches prevent her from rising.

That's what compelled me to climb up and out, and for many of you reading this, I can hear your growl too!

I later realized I didn't rise up only for my son. I'd gain freedom from the chains of disease and dysfunction, not only for my family but for all those willing to glean from what I learned through my journey to wellness.

A Kingdom purpose was birthed to help others heal. A healthy body is required to do and enjoy all God has planned for you. The accomplishment of your own destiny has become part of mine.

It's my joy to show you what worked for me and how it can work for you!

Obstacles don't have to be the end of the story

Stress—including physical, mental, emotional, and spiritual—is a huge part of the disease and dysfunction equation. That, my new friend, is part of what you and I will uncover to reach wholeness and wellness in every area of your life.

My prayer is that you, too, will tear apart every hindrance, keeping you from the life of flourishing abundance you are designed for.

My heartfelt desire is for you to enjoy and be healthfully present, for yourself, for the people in your life you love, and beyond that, for the destiny you're here to fulfill. Its accomplishment requires a spirit, soul, and body that is strong and full of life.

I'm here to tell you my personal story. In doing so, I hope to show you how a brighter day awaits as you hear and apply the message I've been entrusted to carry and pass on.

A life without the restraints of disease and dysfunction is our goal, and we will reach for it together!

Although my experience and credentials speak to the areas in which I'm educated to help those who struggle with overall health, it's God who gives us a Kingdom purpose. He puts the desires in our hearts and the callings He has for our lives.

I can tell you wholeheartedly, I believe the Lord has purposed me to teach people how to live freely, how to connect with their spirit, nourish their souls through that connection, and how to heal their physical bodies as a result.

It's a complete recipe for health and wholeness that I've indulged in, and I'm honored to share that recipe with you!

Our spirit and soul — the foundation for healing

The path toward healing comes from 3 John 1:2 (NLT), "Dear friend, I hope all is well with you and that you are as healthy in body *as* you are strong in spirit." Many translations interchange spirit with soul in this particular Scripture reference.

It's important to understand the direct correlation between being healthy in your body *as* your spirit and soul are strong.

In this book, I'll share what the Lord has taught me about an all-encompassing approach to wellness. Your spirit will be our first focus. As it's positioned to prosper, your soul and body will follow suit.

I'll be introducing you to perhaps the most neglected Person in the church, the Holy Spirit. You may already be familiar with Him, but if your struggles in life are overwhelming you, there's a deeper place with the Holy Spirit I'd like to help usher you into.

The best performance of your life awaits!

The curtain opens with the enabling wisdom and power of Christ. The Holy Spirit sets the stage and is your protagonist through and through.

He's the prominent figure in the theatre of your life, championing you through every scene.

The plot thickens as we dive into soul healing. As with every good story, unexpected twists and turns may arise. The Holy Spirit proves His good character, from beginning to end, as He sees you through. You're held securely in His gentle care as He intertwines Himself with all that is you—your spirit, soul, and body.

By invitation, He will take the role of the award-winning Director He is, leading you in perfect love, counsel, and wisdom.

Emotional healing follows, chock-full of colorful characters from the past. Some are bright, others dark. Each will be addressed with the mind and heart—all with the help of the Holy Spirit.

This progression leads to a robust finale with a body that shines forth refined and functioning at its best—fit and ready to fulfill the Divine destiny it was meant to.

Can you hear the applause? I can.

I'll be with you along the journey to your wellness

I first invite you to sit back and take in my personal story. I'll tell you all about the battle I faced with chronic illness and how I overcame the greatest antagonist of my life.

If I can do it, so can you!

I'll share my struggle with an eating disorder and how I didn't gain victory over this dysfunction in my life until my spirit came into renewal.

I entreat you to gain from the bits of wisdom I found, in the trenches, on my procession to wholeness in spirit, soul, and body.

My hope is that it will champion you to allow the Holy Spirit to take the starring lead role in your own adventure toward a health-filled life story.

Each chapter will end in song and with Heart Connection questions. I encourage you to listen to the lyrics of the songs I've provided, inviting the Holy Spirit to minister to your heart. Then, take the time to introspect with Him as you answer the questions.

They are meant to draw you into a deeper relationship with your Helper, the Holy Spirit.

You'll notice in our journey together that Scripture, taken from the Bible, will be lavishly given. They contain within them the power of God to heal us.

Let's begin with Ephesians 1:17–19. It's a prayer from the Apostle Paul to the church, and it's also my prayer for you. "I keep asking that the God of our Lord Jesus Christ, the glorious Father, may give you the Spirit of wisdom and revelation, so that you may know him better. I pray that the eyes of your heart may be enlightened in order that you may know the hope to which he has called you, the riches of his glorious inheritance in his holy people, and his incomparably great power for us who believe.

Heart Connection

1. Read the lyrics to "Draw Me Close" – Michael W. Smith.[1] I've provided a link for you here: https://www.azlyrics.com/lyrics/ michaelwsmith/drawmeclose.html.

    Are any phrases resonating with you? If so, ask the Holy Spirit what He wants to communicate to you. In a journal, jot down what you hear.

2. Listen to the song "Draw Me Close."[2] I've provided a YouTube link for you here: https://youtu.be/7d_oYr-P16M.

    What else is the Holy Spirit speaking to your heart? Be sure to write it down.

3. Give the Lord thanks for the insight you've been given and for what He is about to do in your life. It's going to be good, *really* good!

4. What is your *why*? What is propelling you to fight disease and dysfunction in your own life?

    Do you believe it's possible to overcome the struggles you're facing? Why or why not?

5. Read John 8:32, "You will know the truth, and the truth will set you free."

    Pray. Ask the Holy Spirit to speak hope and life into your situation and give you the courage to dive deep into His truth, which will set you free!

Part 1
My Story

Chapter 1

The Lupus Octopus

I felt as though I'd been run over by a semi.

Not only from the diagnosis but also from how my body had been limping along over the few weeks prior. I struggled to stay awake more than eight hours in a day. I wasn't just tired; I was fatigued. Evidenced by my rolling out of bed as though I hadn't slept like a log for the last sixteen hours.

I was about to face some rash news

Chronic illness can be like an octopus—each limb represents yet another suffocating symptom and even an additional diagnosis.

I slumped in the chair, taking in the sterile exam room smell every doctor's office carries, and waited to be seen.

I felt a light tap on my shoulder.

"Are you okay?" she asked, squinting as she focused on my eyes.

Awakened from my slumber, I muttered, "Oh wow, yeah, sorry."

Not a typical scene for her, I'm sure. I can't imagine a nineteen-year-old falling asleep on her exam table at their annual gynecological exam was a regular occurrence.

She shifted her blonde hair behind her ear and simultaneously raised her brow, "What's going on here?"

I felt the gentle touch of her hand as she brushed her cool fingers across the bridge of my nose and over my splotchy red cheeks.

I shrugged my shoulder, the very one she had stirred to awaken me.

"You know, I'm not sure. I got a sunburn a few weeks ago, but it won't go away."

I later realized my sun-kissed cheeks had acquired a malar "butterfly" rash[1]—the name fitting to its form and location on my face. My once porcelain skin, now ravaged by the talons of disease, came to be the first arm of the lupus octopus to emerge.

My thyroid came under siege next

Being sick is like having a full-time job. Countless appointments, visiting an array of specialists became my new norm.

After a slew of lab work to discover the cause behind my recent uninvited sleep habits, my gynecologist referred me to an endocrinologist.

I watched the lines on his forehead create even deeper creases as he looked over my lab report.

"With these numbers, I'm surprised you're standing upright at the moment."

I was immediately placed on medication to combat hypo-thyroidism. With this second octopus arm now flailing, I trudged my way up to the checkout desk to make my six-week follow-up appointment.

"Will the same day and time work for you, honey?"

The receptionist received a blank stare in return. I couldn't remember what day it was or the time I'd come in.

Thankfully, as my body soaked up the daily prescribed medication, my impaired memory subsided.[2] Brain fog was another symptom associated with a severely underactive thyroid; it resolved in time, along with the fatigue. Well, mostly.

A sobering diagnosis of lupus soon followed

The doctor I visited next was a rheumatologist, an expert in musculoskeletal disease and autoimmune conditions. He was tall and commanded the room. I sat on the exam table, my feet carelessly dangling, waiting to hear what my lab work and physical exam had revealed this time.

I was only two years out of high school when the news came. I didn't have the slightest clue as to what the doctor's next few words meant.

He pronounced, "You have a positive ANA; let's put you on Plaquenil first and see how you do."

Plaquenil was one of the milder medications I was introduced to early on. All to engage in the battle that began its first rumblings with fatigue and rashes just a few weeks prior.

My young heart was crushed over this unexpected enemy who was armed and ready to subdue my will with new fervor. I was flooded with loads of information I didn't understand—beginning with the antinuclear antibodies found running rampant within my body.

Antibodies are like a well-seasoned army, fighting on our behalf against bacteria, viruses, or any other type of foreign invaders that threaten our body's well-being.[3]

A compromised immune system can mistake the very muscles, joints, tissues, and organs it's intended to defend as the enemy. This confusion causes inflammation and a host of other unwanted symptoms. When an antibody switches allegiance in this way, it's renamed an autoantibody. It defects, forgetting its loyalty to defend and takes on another post, that of the enemy itself.

War had been declared on the friendly soil of my own body.

An antinuclear antibody (ANA) is a type of autoantibody that attacks the protein inside a cell—95 percent of people with lupus will test positive for antinuclear antibodies, but that information alone won't seal a diagnosis.[4]

The American College of Rheumatology (ACR) requires that at least four of the eleven common lupus criteria are met before a firm diagnosis is given.[5] This often leads to patients who suffer for years without a conclusive interpretation of the battle raging within.

I unusually qualified, immediately, with eight presenting symptoms.

The nature of the disease produces various distresses associated with other illnesses, making a diagnosis challenging. It's the "octopus" I was telling you about. These eight-limbed creatures[6] have the reputation of a chameleon, just like lupus.

Octopi blend into their habitat by changing color. Even the intricate patterns they boast on their skeleton-free bodies can be morphed at will.[7] Their ability to camouflage themselves results in making unsuspecting prey their dinner before the victim even realizes it!

Their hide-and-seek technique is often coupled with an inky-black liquid secretion. Disoriented, the imminent meal succumbs to the clutches of the octopus's tentacles and poisonous venom. With a piercing beak, it tears every inch of flesh on its victim into little bite-size pieces.

Welcome to Systemic Lupus Erythematosus (SLE).

Lupus comes from the Latin word for wolf. Its name was coined by the thirteenth-century physician Rogerius who used it to describe erosive facial lesions reminiscent of a wolf's ferocious bite.[8] I'm sure glad I didn't know that tidbit of history when I first found out the disease would come to absorb such a vast part of my own life.

An estimated 1.5 million Americans have been diagnosed with some form of lupus.[9] There are three general types—a discoid form that affects the skin, a drug-induced form caused by certain medications, and a disseminated (systemic) form, which is the kind I was diagnosed with.

The rheumatologist described my situation: "You have an overactive immune system."

I cluelessly blurted out in response, "That's awesome, right? Like, a superhero who heals instantly?"

His eyes widened at my naive assessment. He looked pained in giving his reply.

A tender "not quite" escaped his lips.

As the doctor continued, I realized the accelerated healing powers I imagined for myself were reserved only for fictional comic book characters like Wolverine.

What lay before me was a very real and grave matter, literally. I learned the disease could prove fatal.

Since my immune system was overactive, it attacked not only bad cells but good cells too. It was more of a confused immune system, which wreaked havoc in my life for over 20 years.

The systemic nature of the disease meant it could attack any organ of its diabolical choosing. My lungs, heart, brain, spinal cord, eyes, mouth, skin, muscles, joints, bones, digestive system, reproductive organs, and kidneys were all subject to the ferocious wolf.[10]

No two lupus sufferers are stricken alike, but a commonality they do often share is gender—90 percent of those diagnosed are female.[11]

What is uncommon in lupus when compared to other diseases is that it's more of a roller-coaster ride, characterized by ups and downs, rather than a steady decline in health—although a steady decline has been noted in some patients. Lupus always stands firm to its no two alike character. The only consistency with lupus is its inconsistency.

An increase in disease activity is often referred to as a *flare* followed by times of *remission* where the disease acts dormant. True to the similar attack methods of the elusive octopus.

What in the world is trampling the side of my head?

The latest octopus arm to surface came in the form of a solid slap upside my head.

In my earliest days in the fitness industry, I worked at the front desk of an athletic club. My job was to welcome members with a smile and a small sweat towel.

I loved every part of it—the people, the atmosphere, the encouragement I could extend with only moments and a few simple words.

"Have fun, Joe, you got this!"

"Way to make it in again, Jenny. Enjoy your step class!"

My work shifts flowed with joy and inspiring energy. Then, in its usual unexpected form, lupus trampled in with its latest attack.

It was early in my shift. I suddenly noticed a light show reminiscent of a live concert, for which I hadn't voluntarily purchased a ticket. Lacking color, uninvited, and only visible to myself were floating bright geometrical lines dancing in the fitting shape of lightning bolts on the screen of my right eye.

Attempting to clear the images away, I rubbed both eyes and intermittently pressed my lids together tightly. My efforts proved worthless; the peculiar auras remained.

Suddenly nauseated, I hunkered down, leaning my elbows on the counter. My hands embraced my head firmly as it thundered. I couldn't bear the relentless pounding.

When I opened my eyes, it felt as though I was staring into the blazing sun. I was consumed by the blinding light around me that moments earlier were simply soft rays coming in through the large, picturesque windows of the gym.

It was time to go home.

A migraine unapologetically decimated the day without a moment's notice. Its torment came to visit weekly after this initial display.

Octopi are commonly thought to have eight arms, but marine experts agree that two of its rearmost limbs are, in fact, legs.[12] The next two phases of my lupus experience brought on a burdensome stillness, stopping me dead in my tracks.

Excruciating joint pain was the first phase, my knees and hips took the brunt of the bite, with flares that involved strangling the freedom painless mobility generously permits.

Years later, kidney disease presented as the second leg, preventing the freedom to walk unencumbered in life as I was burdened by a life-sustaining attachment to a dialysis machine—more on that later. For now, my joints had the loudest voice.

Joints fought to move but were denied function

I awoke to the resounding jangle of the telephone bellowing from the other room. Cell phones weren't the norm back then. My only means of communication with the outside world was linked to a physical wire connected to the far wall of our sunflower-decorated kitchen.

With the insistent ring of the phone, and screaming joints voicing their vexation at the immune attack directed at them, I begrudgingly rolled out of bed and toppled onto the carpet, whiffing its staleness. Crawling about like an inchworm, I hoisted myself up on the kitchen counter, despite the shrill protests coming from my inflamed joints.

Finally. Breathlessly, I answered, "Hello?"

Then, there were stairs, the most exhausting of feats to conquer. Not only for myself but for the family members who reached up from behind, lacing their arms underneath my armpits, to bear the weight of my frame onto their capable bodies. Only then could I endure the seemingly endless flight of stairs that led to my beckoning bedroom.

My legs weren't the only joints affected. Fingers, wrists, elbows, and shoulders shared in the torture. Thankfully, with heavy medications onboard, this brutal flare subsided. In fact, I had a reprieve from lupus altogether and was in remission for the next several years.

Soon, I was even pregnant!

Sleep became my greatest unfulfilled longing

It was a week before delivery, and I hadn't slept for a solid three days. My first bout with dreadful insomnia came knocking on my weary soul. For some reason, my normal sleep pattern was severely disrupted. In fact, I didn't have a sleep pattern at all!

Not a single wink graced my dreary eyes.

My best friend, Kitty, was tender and motherly, always welcoming, and ready to serve in any way possible. She was the type who made sure you were well-fed, whether hungry or not. She wasn't even Italian!

Her prayers were always full of compassion. It wasn't uncommon for her to cry as she lifted the cares of others to the Lord. We had our very own two-person Bible study every Thursday morning. Just Kitty and me. It was the best part of my week, and the fact that she lived within walking distance from my house was the best part of my neighborhood.

I called her in desperation. "Kitty, I don't know what's wrong. I can't sleep!"

Within minutes she was at my doorstep. Gently laying her hand on mine, she prayed. "Father, thank you that you love your daughter. Help her to rest and get the sleep she needs. In Jesus' name, I pray. Amen."

I wailed in her arms as she held me close, unconvinced another prayer would make a difference. I'd been praying for days myself.

Worrying about not falling asleep only made matters worse, but I couldn't help myself. Sitting straight up in bed, on the verge of hyperventilating, I remembered a Tom and Jerry cartoon episode from my youth.

Tom, the cat, had bloodshot eyes. Curved toothpicks, shaking from the pressure, were the only barrier keeping his top and bottom eyelids from collapsing onto each other. I couldn't recall the reason for Tom needing toothpicks to keep his eyelids open. I imagine Jerry, the mouse, was up to his usual antics and the likely culprit.

I, too, felt like a cat run ragged. My own eyes equally inflamed and irritated just as Tom's had been. Though I was exhausted, there was no respite in sight.

I ached for a good night's rest. At this point, even a short nap would do. The minute my head hit the pillow, my pulse raced instead. After three days of this madness, my water broke unexpectedly.

About 30 percent of babies whose mothers have lupus are born prematurely.[13] My Nathan was no exception. He was five weeks early—all four pounds of him.

My tiny baby made his big entrance into the world

The first ten days of Nathan's little life were spent in the Neonatal Intensive Care Unit. While other preemies needed oxygen, Nathan didn't. I guess he figured he'd make a proud momma out of me from the get-go.

Little did he know, there was nothing required of him to make me proud. I just was, and always would be. No matter what. That kid belonged to me; he was mine! The love I felt was like no other I'd experienced before; it was unconditional.

Could this be how God loved me? After all, I was His.

I treasured the insight the Lord was imparting to my heart as I cradled my one and only son. I thought about how God also had a One and only, Jesus.

I marveled at how He sacrificed Him for me so that I could be in a relationship with Him. I felt in harmony with God, at peace with the world.

Later, I came across this gem from God's Word. "His left arm is under my head, and his right arm embraces me" (Song of Solomon 2:6).

I went from peaceful to frenzied only a few hours later

I had hoped after giving birth that a regular sleep cycle would reemerge.

Instead, I was worse.

Is it the lack of sleep that has me on pins and needles?

I jumped at the sound of the phone, ringing next to the hospital bed. Each successive ring registered as a shrill alarm. The exasperation felt too much to bear; I called for my nurse.

I asked, "Is this postpartum stuff?"

She wrapped a blood pressure cuff tightly above my elbow, level with my racing heart. I felt it strangle my arm. My own lungs were feeling a similar type of suffocation.

I was caught up in mental torment with unrelenting thoughts circling like vultures on a feeding frenzy. I couldn't focus. I heard the nurse talking, but her words seemed to float away before I could register them.

Was she telling me what my blood pressure was? I pressed in to listen.

"Mimi, are you having thoughts of harming yourself or someone else?"

Avoiding the first part of her question, I shot back, "Of course not! Why would I hurt someone else?"

"And what about you, dear. Do you want to hurt yourself?"

I mean, sure, I did feel if my life would be marked with this level of mental turmoil that I'd rather not be alive, but I had a baby to take care of now.

Suicide was absolute crazy talk!

Still, I was covered in a commotion of emotions I couldn't control or explain.

Why was I feeling so shaky?

I looked down at my fingers to see if they mimicked what was happening on the inside. Surely, they'd be trembling too. Somehow, they weren't.

I placed my hand over my chest.

Was my heartbeat audible?

It felt like it should be.

Extreme thoughts continued tumbling through my mind, without a single outward confirmation about what was going on within. What was the cause of this unwarranted mayhem?

Someone, help me. Please!

Heart Connection

1. Read the lyrics to "Jesus the One and Only" – Brooklyn Tabernacle Choir.[14] I've provided a link for you here: https://www.musixmatch. com/lyrics/Brooklyn-Tabernacle-Choir/Jesus-The-One-And-Only.

    Are any phrases resonating with you? If so, ask the Holy Spirit what He wants to communicate to you. In a journal, jot down what you hear.

2. Listen to the song "Jesus the One and Only."[15] I've provided a YouTube link for you here: https://youtu.be/oCSVNSi-UzY.

    What else is the Holy Spirit speaking to your heart? Be sure to write it down.

3. Do you see yourself as a child of God? Read 1 John 3:1 (ESV), "See what kind of love the Father has given us, that we should be called children of God; and so we are."

    If you've never considered this to be true for you, ask the Holy Spirit to impart it to you now. If you know your position as a child of God already, ask the Holy Spirit to bring you into a deeper place of revelation.

4. When you consider your relationship with God, do you feel His love for you is unconditional? Why or why not? Ask the Holy Spirit to show you how much God loves you.

5. What trials have you gone through with chronic illness? What are you currently experiencing with regard to your health? Ask the Holy Spirit to comfort you.

Chapter 2

Pain from the Past

I couldn't breathe.

Maybe I was experiencing new mom anxiety? After all, I was never around children. I had zero experience. While most teens had babysitting jobs, my work involved being a janitor. Truth be told, not only did I lack a background in caring for other children, I had little opportunity to be one myself.

My parents are first-generation immigrants to the U.S. In fact, my dad's entire extended family still lives in Argentina. My mom comes from Sicily, bringing along her master cooking skills. Homemade fresh baked bread, pasta with its accompanying red sauce, and Italian sweets are her specialty.

Too much work and not enough fun

Neither one of my parents spoke English as they embarked on making a living in a different culture and country. We all worked hard to make money—my dad more than anyone. He slaved from morning to night providing for us and making ends meet.

His full-time day job was at a hospital as a maintenance man. His daily tasks included changing light bulbs, fixing loose latches on doors, and taking care of all the other odds and ends needing attention throughout the hospital.

Even though he was hard-working, reliable, and friendly, he was paid little and rarely got a raise. At sixteen years old, my starting wage at a retail store was more than his, and he'd been working at the hospital for eight years by then. He couldn't advocate for himself because of the language barrier, and they took advantage of that.

The hospital was a forty-minute drive from our home. As a result, my dad was awake before the sun came up. His workday began at five thirty in the morning. After a tiring eight-hour shift, he'd come home, eat one of Mom's scrumptious Italian dinners, and take a refueling thirty-minute siesta in preparation for his second job.

Then, we all went to work as a family.

It hurt to watch others play while I worked

I remember my childhood being much different than the kids in the neighborhood.

From afar, I watched as other little girls got dressed up for their dance recitals, gymnastics meets, or laced up their special sneakers set aside for softball or soccer games.

All the while, I went to work.

Our entire evenings were consumed with cleaning office buildings. One, in particular, was an optical company with a large industrial area for the production of eyeglass lenses.

My dad had to use a garden hose to wash down the cement; then he scrubbed every inch of the floor with a heavy-duty broom. The stiff soap-filled fibers, combined with my dad's muscle power, brought it from filthy to fabulous in no less than a couple of hours.

I can still picture him wiping the sweat from his brow before taking on the floor squeegee. He'd push the grungy water down drains located between large pieces of production equipment. It was messy work and tiresome.

While my dad took care of the factory floor, we tag-teamed the rest. My mom, brother, and I dumped ashtrays and trash. It wasn't fun wiping the grimy ashtrays or smelling trash all night, but we made the best of it. Sometimes, there'd be candy dishes on people's desks! We took delight in a mini chocolate bar or Jolly Rancher whenever we could.

My mom and I scrubbed toilets and restocked empty hand-towel dispensers and toilet paper bins. Sometimes she'd catch me singing made-up songs or working on my latest Madonna or Michael Jackson moves.

When my brother got big and strong enough, he strapped a backpack vacuum over his shoulders and snuffed out any debris from the carpeted areas in the offices and storage rooms; once I could reach up high, I was in charge of making doors sparkle and restroom mirrors shine.

That was my life, from the age of eight and up until I got married. I would have rather been dancing in a sequin tutu, somersaulting on a gym floor mat, or batting softballs out of the park while making childhood friends along the way.

It wasn't an option for me, and deep down, that really hurt.

I wouldn't know how much until years later when I worked through the pain of having lived through a very different type of childhood.

Two clashing cultures brought more heartache

My parents suffered in their own ways and had zero tolerance when it came to anything that didn't align with their views or expectations.

I imagine working long days with exhausting work, from morning to night, for little financial return was a part of the reason for their short fuses and physical outbursts. As a result, fear entered my life and the idea that perfection would keep me safe and out of trouble cemented in my soul.

Coming from an old-world background, my parents were adamant that I not speak to boys. Dating was completely out of the question. I had different ideas but wasn't allowed to express my opinion. My freedom was stifled, and intentions questioned as innocent as they were.

Any expression of negative emotion or disagreement with their rules was unacceptable. There was no room to disagree with their set ideals.

I didn't have a voice.

I learned that not complying with expectations meant serious consequences. They viewed harsh discipline as a badge of honor. In their minds, they'd be doing something wrong if they didn't keep the reins tight. Sometimes, even mistakes resulted in punishment.

I was born into one culture but lived in another. I wanted to experience the latter, but the two couldn't be reconciled in my parents' eyes. They were like oil and vinegar.

I desperately wanted the life and freedom American kids had. Their discipline involved being grounded or a privilege taken away. I could only dream of such an easy consequence.

They were allowed to wear makeup and have slumber parties. They were permitted to have friends that were boys without suspecting something bad was going on.

They didn't have to work for a living; they got to be kids.

There was always more work to do

My responsibilities continued to grow with each passing year.

My dad wasn't the only one with multiple jobs. Janitorial work served as my second one, too, since I took schoolwork very seriously and considered it my first. I learned to prioritize wisely, doing homework assignments immediately after school. There'd be no time to study in the evening.

Homework was stressful and took time to complete since my parents couldn't help with most of my questions. Math was the exception because of its universal language. My dad was terrific at math and was always willing to help, despite his long days.

Interestingly, math was my weakest subject. Perhaps it was because I got the help I needed right away. I didn't have to dig and search for answers. For other subjects, I was forced to go on a solitary hunting expedition. In those days, Google and Siri weren't yet available to come to the rescue.

I discovered the things I had to work more earnestly for ended up producing perseverance, and brought about a learning process that formed lasting fruit. Romans 5:3–4 (NLT) defined my experience perfectly, "We can rejoice, too, when we run into problems and trials, for we know that they help us develop endurance. And endurance develops strength of character, and character strengthens our confident hope of salvation."

I'd experience this firsthand once again, on my journey to health and wellness, later in life.

In my early school days, a program was implemented called "the homework hotline." I was able to call a volunteer teacher who answered my most difficult questions. As I think back at how I sought help in completing assignments, I'm grateful a resource like the homework hotline became available. It was a Godsend before I even knew who God was personally.

His promises were sure, without my recognition. When I later discovered Psalm 23:1 (NLT), "The LORD is my shepherd; I have all that I need," I knew it had been true for me throughout my childhood and going forward.

Although I was forced to grow up before I had the chance to really be a kid, I was certain the Lord had guided and provided for me throughout each step. All the while, a strength of character was being produced in me that I may have never gained had I not been placed in the circumstances I found myself in.

Burdened with too much responsibility

As it turns out, I ended up with more than two jobs. In high school, I worked weekends at Kmart. I was a hostess to customers wanting to use the fitting room to try clothes on. I also organized merchandise and reticketed apparel clearance items.

My favorite part was making flashing blue light special announcements. Once I got going, they couldn't peel the intercom from my hands. All to pay for the fire-engine red Geo Storm car I purchased; I loved zipping around town in that car.

School, janitorial work, and a retail job were more than enough responsibility for a young person, but I had another one still. Naturally, I was required to interpret.

We only spoke Italian and Spanish in our home. I came into kindergarten without a single English word in my vocabulary. With full immersion in school, I learned quickly, and my knowledge was frequently put to use by my parents.

As a child, I wrote checks and made phone calls to doctors, insurance, and bill companies. My diabetic grandmother lived with us, too, so I went to both her and my parents' doctor's appointments to interpret.

I didn't realize, at the time, how burdened I was in carrying all that responsibility. Eventually, it took its toll, affecting my physical body. I've learned throughout my healing journey that our heartaches can't be discounted. Whether big or small, the reality of our experiences must be processed.

Acknowledgment of things we've gone through makes for a whole and healthy person. Affirming our experiences, rather than denying them, is important and crucial in overcoming disease and dysfunction in our lives.

Your childhood may have looked different than mine, but most of us have areas of pain that must be brought out of hiding and exposed to the healing light of the Holy Spirit's wisdom.

I invite you to begin exploring with Him, in the Heart Connection questions, at the end of each chapter. You'll have an opportunity to dive deeper into Holy Spirit led soul healing in Chapter 17.

The working of everything for good

In the meantime, rest in the promise of Romans 8:28, "And we know that in *all things God works for the good* of those who love him, who have been called according to his purpose."

Looking back, I know that *all things* were for my gain. The unsolicited charge to be responsible for things beyond my years, while growing up in a culturally different home, worked a future glory I get to walk in today.

I acquired excellent communication skills by having conversations with adults at a young age. I'm a speaker today and love conveying truth to others through my experiences. Being able to speak life into multiple cultures because I'm trilingual is another *good* thing. Oh, and I've learned to make my mom's Italian sweet treats! That's good for everyone, according to my husband.

I may have been weighed down with a lot of work growing up, but what I get to do today doesn't seem like work at all. Mark Twain had it right when he said, "If you love what you do, you'll never work another day in your life."[1]

As a personal trainer, I've had times when I've chased my clients around the track to motivate them to run. I get to create workout routines that are life-giving and fun. I've changed people's lives for the better with nutritional guidance and behavior change sessions, led by the Holy Spirit. I found what I was created for, my Kingdom purpose!

All the friendships I missed out on growing up don't compare to the friends I have now. My clients are some of them!

God uses every circumstance in our lives to draw us into greater intimacy with Him as we seek answers. In receiving them, He becomes our Best Friend of all time.

I'm grateful as I see the hand of God in my life today, not despite my childhood, but because of it. God doesn't author the pain, but He will use it for a purpose in His Kingdom if you allow it.

This working of *good* isn't just for me; it's for you too!

As you explore your past realities with the Holy Spirit, He will bring forth truth, healing, and perhaps, your very own Kingdom purpose.

Heart Connection

1. Read the lyrics to "Intentional" – Travis Greene.[2] I've provided a link for you here: https://www.azlyrics.com/lyrics/travisgreene/intentional.html.

   Are any phrases resonating with you? If so, ask the Holy Spirit what He wants to communicate to you. In a journal, jot down what you hear.

2. Listen to the song "Intentional."[3] I've provided a YouTube link for you here: https://www.youtube.com/watch?v=VH3foellNv8.

   What else is the Holy Spirit speaking to your heart? Be sure to write it down.

3. Do you recognize pain rooted in your childhood?

   Ask the Holy Spirit to meet you where you are in this moment as you recall the events and people involved. Talk to Him about your feelings. Be honest. He understands; He was there.

4. Ask the Holy Spirit if there are any lies you believe as a result of the pain. Then ask Him to reveal what the truth is. Write it down and meditate on the truth you've been given.

5. Ask the Holy Spirit to speak to you about the good that came from the situation. Thank Him for working all things together for good, in His perfect timing.

Chapter 3

The Psych Ward

I paced the lobby, waiting for the psychiatrist to call me into her office.

My eyes were glued to my son as he slept. Nathan was cozily tucked in the red-and-blue plaid car seat we received as a baby shower gift.

I marveled at how tiny he looked in it and thought about how the hospital wouldn't release him until he made weight. He came home at exactly five pounds—appropriately, the weight of a bag of sugar.

I wanted to be a great mom. More than anything, my desire was for him to experience a real childhood—*Leave it to Beaver* style if possible, chock-full of every kind of sitcom-worthy shenanigans.

I thought about him playing piano someday or running around bases during a little league team practice. His interests would become my first priority. I wanted him to have every opportunity I didn't.

With illness crowding in on every front, I was concerned. Was I capable of taking care of his needs? I wondered if that thought, coupled with my lack of experience with anything child related, was the reason behind the anxiety.

I told myself everything would work out. Still, my soul refused to rest.

Before leaving the delivery ward, I was placed on anxiety and depression medication. My instructions were to visit a psychiatrist as soon as I could get scheduled.

Hope was followed by the unthinkable

The receptionist *finally* called my name.

"Mimi?"

I scrambled to grab my things.

This wasn't the typical doctor's office I was used to visiting. I entered an actual office rather than a patient room and noticed a picture of a serene meadow on the wall. An inviting, oversized chair sat catty-corner to the psychiatrist's desk. The doctor had a calm way about her, and I watched as she glided toward her seat.

She motioned for me to take mine directly in front of her.

Her voice was soothing, "How are you doing today, Mimi?"

I wanted to say, *"Clearly, I'm a mess! Can't you see I came in my pajamas?"*

They were the same ones I'd been living in for the past two weeks since the delivery. The anxiety continued to gain traction in the days after leaving the hospital. It was all-consuming, relentlessly knocking on the door of my mind and emotions.

I still wasn't sleeping. The constant worry paired up with a beastly depression and left no room for conversations, even with

God. It felt like the devil had finally won. He took from me the one thing I'd always found rest in: prayer.

The entanglement of anxiety and depression was worse than any physical pain I'd ever endured. My thoughts were cluttered, piled to the top in a heap of mental anguish. The black hole of depression zapped all human desire from me. My emotions were heightened, and yet I was simultaneously numb.

I wanted to answer the psychiatrist's question honestly but replied with my usual, "I'm fine, thanks."

Unconvinced, she went on to describe a spa-like adventure, prepared just for me.

"We'd like to help you relax and get the help you need."

I was doubtful anything could pull me out of this pit. I looked down at my pathetic frayed slippers as she continued.

"You won't have to worry about your baby, everything will be taken care of for you, and we can look into why you're feeling this way."

Her offer sounded reasonable enough. I'd do just about anything to get a bit of relief from the torment of thoughts swirling in my mind and the depression draining any ounce of vitality I once had.

Maybe, I'll start to get some sleep too?

I felt ill-equipped for motherhood, and my current mental status only confirmed my insecurities. Physically, I began experiencing some joint pain as well.

Ugh, not again, I thought.

I massaged my aching knee as I considered the option set before me.

If I could get help in caring for Nathan while getting my mind and body back in harmony, why wouldn't I?

I felt a bit of hope rise up and agreed, but the small glimmer of light soon darkened.

I didn't realize I had signed my life away

I found myself at a different hospital than the one I'd just delivered Nathan in.

I mindlessly signed paperwork the intake administrator had for me.

No one reads this stuff anyway, right?

I was getting good at multitasking, cradling Nathan while filling out the forms.

A nurse interrupted, "Mimi, it's time to say goodbye to your baby."

Wait, what? Did I miss something here?

Dazed at being confronted with the unimaginable, I shot up from my chair.

"The psychiatrist said I'd get help in caring for my baby, not have him taken from me!"

I realized after talking further with the nurse that I had unknowingly signed myself into a mental hospital!

A burst of emotion followed. Over and over, I repeated the same words.

"I'm not staying here without my baby, *please*! I don't want to be here. I don't *need* to be here. I want to go home!"

All of my begging was met with apathy and accomplished nothing.

Fully composed, the nurse responded to my cries.

"I'm sorry, you can't leave without permission from a doctor."

Her calmness only highlighted my contrasting shrills, confirming the perception I belonged there.

More binding than my burst of emotion were the signed papers that lay before me. My fate had been sealed with ink by the stroke of my own hand.

This supposed place of ease and refreshment had become my prison.

Industrial-sized metal doors contained small square windows; behind them, faces bobbed back and forth as they swayed for comfort. I passed by an unoccupied room and noticed mismatched baby-blue and pink curtains and two twin-size beds with small shabby desks adjacent to them.

This room was nothing like the labor and delivery room I'd just been in, or like any of the other hospital rooms I'd visited in all my lupus years. It reminded me of an abandoned college dorm room in the summer months, void of any semblance of life.

Perfect. Exactly how I was feeling.

Since only a doctor's approval could bail me out, I asked to speak to one.

"I'm sorry, that's not possible. We don't have a doctor here right now."

I didn't believe her, but what could I do? I was trapped. Even though my thinking was cluttered, I knew one thing, I was getting out!

I imagined Nathan at home cuddled up with his Millie, the rainbow-colored caterpillar-stuffed animal I'd purchased while setting up the nursery.

My mind drifted to his room, freshly stenciled with bears around the perimeter and matching bedding. I knew my place was in the rocking chair we positioned next to his crib for midnight feedings.

I don't belong here!

I was forced to stay but refused medications

I was relieved they didn't shove me in the eerie room I noticed on my way in. Although, where I ended up didn't seem much better.

They placed me in a small windowless room. I heard the lock engage as the door shut firmly.

Eventually, an overly friendly nurse popped in; she was all smiles. There was something off about her; I knew she couldn't be trusted.

"Why isn't there a phone in here?" I asked angrily.

My outburst slid right off her. Still smiling, she insisted I take the tiny green pill she brought in with her, "This will make you feel better."

She was offering a potent antipsychotic drug. If I took it, I knew it would bring about a stupor I couldn't afford. Nothing was going to dull my determination to get back to my son.

I refused, without a moment's hesitation.

I could tell the nurse was seasoned at her job. She made it seem as though she cared and was on my side, but I could sense her lack of sympathy and detachment. She continued pressing me to take the medication. I found out later that the drug is commonly used to treat schizophrenia.

We went back and forth in conversation like opponents in a ping-pong match. There was no way she was winning. She was up against a new momma bear, and I'd find my way back to my cub, no matter what.

I scooted back in the chair and then dragged it closer to the nurse, maintaining unwavering eye contact.

I gave her my final match spin, "Stop telling me you know what will help me! I'm not taking that poison. Now, get out!"

I could feel an angry cry coming on as I pointed my finger at the door.

I wasn't proud of how I was acting, but all I could think about was avoiding being added to their list of patients who bobbed back and forth, devoid of all human emotion.

I kept telling myself I was strong, that it wouldn't be my fate. I'd get through this; I had to.

What's happening to me; why do I feel this way?

I think many people think about suicide without any real intention of following through. That was my situation, at least. Most people don't talk about their suicidal thoughts because it's scary and sharing vulnerable feelings with someone else, even more frightening.

I had no idea another reason would be forced residence in a mental facility! As I wrestled with my current circumstances, I thought about Elijah, in the Old Testament, of the Bible.

Didn't he run away, sit under a tree, and pray for death? " 'I have had enough, Lord,' he said. 'Take my life; I am no better than my ancestors' " (1 Kings 19:4).

Ditto, my feelings exactly.

The Apostle Paul shared similar sentiments in 2 Corinthians 1:8, "We do not want you to be uninformed, brothers and sisters, about the troubles we experienced in the province of Asia. We were under great pressure, far beyond our ability to endure, so that we despaired of life itself."

It seemed that my desire to give up, even to the point of suicide, was somewhat of a natural response to unbearable difficulty.

My parents came to the rescue

My parents were told where I was, likely by the administrators at the hospital. They rushed to my rescue immediately. They were unfamiliar with this hospital, and their English was still poor. Yet, they were able to figure out how to get to me.

They believed I could get through the current obstacle set before me without being separated from my family and inundated with sedating drugs. In fact, they were a huge part of imparting the kind of fortitude it takes to make it in life, despite barriers.

I gained resilience through the hardship of growing up all too quickly. As a result of their living in a culture they couldn't freely operate in, we all gained strength. I rose to the challenges and took care of things they weren't able to do for themselves. I'm not saying it was easy or even what I wanted, but I do believe it made me the strong person I became. I was capable and resilient.

Now, my parents were fighting for me. I realized they had been all along. They came through for me, even with the language barrier and their limited resources. They defiantly parked themselves at the nurse's station, refusing to leave until I was allowed to go home.

Latinos and Italians aren't known to be quiet people. A generalization, perhaps, but it describes my family perfectly. The hospital staff was forced to contact the doctor on call. I was released just before midnight, provided I'd attend a suicide prevention program for the next few weeks.

Learning to acknowledge and deal with pain

I was thankful I'd been rescued from the hospital and felt more settled as I looked forward to group sessions consisting of others who had contemplated suicide in the recent past. Eight of us sat in a circle on uncomfortable metal folding chairs, matching exactly how I felt on the inside.

This was awkward.

The instructor spoke gently; his eyes communicated kindness and understanding. I could tell he was intentional about making eye contact with each one of us as he walked around the inner circle. I began to feel more at ease, deciding he genuinely cared.

I leaned in to listen.

"The most important thing to remember is to call a friend."

That seemed simple enough. If thoughts of suicide came, my go-to would be to contact someone for help.

He then asked us to make a list of people who might be willing to be there for us if the need should arise. I wrote seven names down in a flash and thought about how grateful I was to have so many caring people in my life I could trust with my feelings.

Compassion filled my heart as I watched some of the other participants struggling with their lists. I wondered if it might be the very reason they were part of this circle now. Certainly, loneliness is disheartening and can lead to despair.

In later days, we learned about processing our emotions and digging deep into the reasons we were feeling desperate enough to consider suicide.

As I suspected, fear was the big one for me.

I wasn't sure I'd be the mom I wanted to be. My need for perfection, based on my rigid childhood, fueled that fear. The reality of sneak attacks from the octopus burned in my subconscious as well. Even if I wasn't sick, I didn't know how to be a mom. It was all so new and scary.

I thought my fears and inadequacies could be alleviated, most easily, by not having to confront them at all. My absence was a sure way to gain immediate relief. That was the only reason I could come up with for wanting to give up on life, but more insight soon came.

A lupus protocol with pros and cons

I'd been given massive doses of a steroid medication during my delivery. It's a preventative measure, often dispensed to lupus patients, to alleviate a possible flare from childbirth stress. It turns out that I had an adverse reaction to the amount of medication administered—the steroids were the cause of much of my post-birth mental gymnastics.

It's common for steroids, especially in large doses, to cause problematic psychiatric conditions.[1] I only understood this was part of the anxiety, depression, and suicidal thoughts I had experienced, when two decades later, I was given the same drug and reacted in like manner.

The medication did its job as far as reducing the inflammation in my body. Once the dose was reduced, I enjoyed motherhood and a body that functioned relatively free of major flares for the next twenty-one years.

A lot happened during those reprieve-filled years

The octopus was largely silent as I watched Nathan go from goldfish crackers and naps in kindergarten to pizza parties and high school volleyball games. I was grateful for Nathan's dad, who picked up the slack and cared for me selflessly throughout our marriage, especially whenever I experienced small flare-ups of fatigue, insomnia, and migraines that persisted.

I'd been married for fifteen years to the most compassionate and faithful friend I could have asked for. Sadly, I made some poor choices, rooted in the pain I carried from childhood. We parted ways, and by God's grace, I later met Ben.

From the get-go, Ben and I realized how much we had in common—a love of fitness, to be sure, but also a sense of history. Our first conversation, in fact, was his travel to Italy and Argentina, the birthplaces of my parents.

We began dating and soon fell hopelessly in love. So much seemed to be going right after the pain of divorce. Though relatively unseen, the octopus was increasing in strength. Lupus was undetectably gaining ground, consuming my kidneys, and causing irreversible damage.

That's when the other leg of the octopus curled out of hiding and made itself known.

Heart Connection

1. Read the lyrics to "Peace Be Still" – Lauren Daigle.[2] I've provided a link for you here: https://www.azlyrics.com/lyrics/belongingco/peacebestill.html.

    Are any phrases resonating with you? If so, ask the Holy Spirit what He wants to communicate to you. In a journal, jot down what you hear.

2. Listen to the song "Peace Be Still."[3] I've provided a YouTube link for you here: https://youtu.be/VBzg4B3_yS8.

    What else is the Holy Spirit speaking to your heart? Be sure to write it down.

3. Have there been times, throughout your journey, when you've experienced anxiety, depression, or suicidal thoughts? How did you cope? Did friends or family members come alongside you to help? If you feel it's appropriate, write them a thank you note.

4. Are you currently experiencing anxiety over the situations you find yourself in?

    Read Philippians 4:6–7, "Do not be anxious about anything, but in every situation, by prayer and petition, with thanksgiving, present your requests to God. And the peace of God, which transcends all understanding, will guard your hearts and minds in Christ Jesus."

    Pray. Ask God for your heart's desires and for help in aligning your thoughts with the promises in His Word. Thank Him in advance for what He is about to do in your life. Allow His peace to fill your heart as you believe.

5. Read and meditate on Romans 15:13, "May the God of hope fill you with all joy and peace *as you trust in him,* so that you may overflow with hope by the power of the Holy Spirit."

    Ask the Holy Spirit to impart the truth of this Scripture to your heart. If we lack joy and peace, then our trust level needs to increase! Ask Him to show you how you can better trust Him and then do what He's guiding you to do.

Chapter 4

Kidney Disease & Chemotherapy

It was the ultimate flare-up.

It was the kind of flare I hadn't experienced in more than two decades. Every joint was screaming and demanding my attention.

"Joshy, will you please pull on my sleeve?" I grimaced.

The fitted sweatshirts, I was used to wearing, were now a huge challenge to maneuver out of on my own.

"Sure, Meems, I got it."

Josh was a personal training client I met shortly after my divorce. He quickly became a good friend. No one was more mellow than him and I felt a sense of peace and comfort when I was around him. He had become like a brother to me, with his sympathetic smile and supportive ways. A rock in the aftermath of my divorce, and now this.

Before long, I was shopping for loose clothing and arthritic pain creams. A few weeks later, I found myself in the hospital, the joint pain worse than ever, and a splitting migraine taking center stage.

That is until a more pressing matter took front and center.

In the hospital with devastating news to come

All my senses were heightened. The dimmest light boasted itself brighter than it really was. My ears were sensitive to the faintest sound, and I could still smell the buttermilk pancakes on the breakfast tray brought in hours earlier.

Why wasn't the migraine medication kicking in?

Writhing in pain, I silently begged to be taken out of my skin.

Please, God, I want to die! Take me home.

Thoughts of suicide and anxiety, long forgotten, found their way back. The result of high-dose steroids, once again.

Undoubtedly, my pleas were also brought on by the continual pummeling of the entire left side of my head. Even with earplugs, every sound seemed to be magnified as though a blaring air horn was firmly situated inches from my face.

My pulsating eye throbbed without reprieve, while tears seeped beneath the bottom rim of my eye mask and trickled down my chin. A migraine was vying for a takeover, but something more serious was getting ready to take charge.

A new reality with dire consequences

The latest expert I became familiar with was a nephrologist. He knew all things kidney. I liked him; he was caring but meant business. He reminded me of how I handled the wellness clients under my own care.

Since the beginning, lupus threatened the proper functioning of my kidneys. I was being monitored over the years and didn't have a reason for too much concern—until this hospital visit.

I didn't realize the severity of what was happening; it was clear now.

The task at hand was to save my life.

Who knew kidneys played such a huge role in keeping the human body in harmony? Thankfully, my nephrologist did.

He made his way to the steely hospital bed I'd been borrowing for the last several days. He spoke quietly, "Mimi, it's Dr. Schlessinger."

My attention was drawn out from the chaos within. I removed the earplugs to hear him more clearly.

"Mimi, I'd like to do a biopsy of your kidneys."

I had refused the procedure before, fearing infection, since my immune system was so compromised. Dr. S. made it clear it was necessary, at this point, to determine treatment going forward.

The migraine and joint pain subsided in time, but the biopsy showed extensive permanent damage to both kidneys.

Deadly chemicals interspersed with an undying love

I reluctantly agreed to undergo chemotherapy in an attempt to stem the onslaught of kidney disease, provoked by my overactive immune system.

Much like a tumor decreases in size under treatment, the same approach was taken to help diminish the upsurge of autoantibodies at war inside my body. The goal was to spare my kidneys.

Dr. Schlessinger became integral in my care from that point forward. Other doctors also weaved in and out, taking charge of their particular specialty as needed.

An oncologist was next on the scene.

To begin, I chose a less potent type of chemotherapy, mostly because I was told I wasn't likely to lose my hair.

I know, shallow, right?

Not really, just human.

Six months later, with hair intact and kidneys worse, I succumbed to stronger chemotherapy.

With a sunken heart, I questioned the oncologist.

"Will I lose my hair this time?"

His reply gave little comfort, "It's a low dose, so you may not."

It certainly didn't feel like a low dose. With every treatment, I was tossed to-and-fro on a sea of overwhelming nausea, even with pills onboard promising otherwise.

My crumbling kidneys were too weak to filter out the extra fluid from the IV bags. I watched as my hands, stomach, legs, and ankles inflated like a brimful water balloon.

Ben lovingly pressed his lips on my plump hands, and in his best *Addams Family* Gomez voice teased, "I always wanted a chubby Italian girl," traveling up my arm with every kiss.

Apparently, he meant it.

When he proposed—in the midst of chemo treatments, causing my hair to thin and my body to inflate—I said yes.

I'd be crazy not to.

It was true love!

Holding on to faith through it all

I hated the idea of dangerous chemicals seeping throughout every inch of my body. As a believer in God's promises, I relied heavily on a Scripture from Mark 16:18a NLT, "They will be able to handle snakes with safety, *and if they drink anything poisonous, it won't hurt them.*"

With every piercing twinge caused by inserted needles, tiresome aches, stabbing headaches, and all the other side effects from the very medications that were intended to make me feel better, I was reminded of the Scriptures I placed my hope in, but they weren't *feeling* very true.

I was believing and yet not seeing; the very definition of faith according to the Bible, "Now faith is confidence in what we hope for and assurance about what we do not see" (Hebrews 11:1).

What I was going through was attempting to overpower the truth of God's Word regarding healing, but I was determined to hold on to it despite my circumstances.

An IV drip was pinned to my arm, pumping medication through my veins. Every three weeks, there I sat, in the company of fellow sufferers, swallowed up in a gargantuan recliner that could house three of me.

The extra space proved to be useful as I simultaneously took in spiritual medication, which I knew could strengthen me during the wait. Devotionals, books written by Christian authors, and the Word of God itself consumed every available crevice around me.

I kept telling myself I'd be healed, even if my present circumstances dictated otherwise.

When it didn't seem like anything was happening outwardly, friends stepped in along the way, making me aware that God was still at work.

Friends became the face and hands of God

The oncologist who took charge of the chemotherapy part of my care instructed me, "You'll be given some sedating medication and will need someone to drive you home from treatments."

I dreaded asking for help.

That was one of the mindsets I later learned to give up in my quest toward wholeness. During this time, I still lived with my childhood deception that I had to do everything myself.

Not wanting to burden the same people, I called one of the worship leaders from my church. She had an angelic voice, matched only in tone by her powerhouse ability to soothe an anxious heart with her calm demeanor.

My heart raced, "Hi, Kelly, can you take me to my next chemo treatment?"

I let out a sigh waiting for her answer, hoping she wouldn't hear it over the phone.

"Of course, I'll take you, thanks for asking me." Her reply caught me by surprise.

Did she just thank me for asking her?

The apprehension I felt immediately left at her gracious response. I began to realize I didn't have to fight this octopus, on my own, or anything else life brought my way.

I had long since learned God could be trusted to be there for me. My life experiences and Scriptures, like Psalm 16:8, had always reassured me: "I keep my eyes always on the LORD. With him at my right hand, I will not be shaken."

It was healing to realize people were happily willing to help during the shakings too. I was learning it was okay to ask for help when I needed it, without fear or shame.

The chemotherapy process left me weary

I sat on my tiny apartment patio, journaling my prayers to God. Writing kept me focused, especially when I dealt with anxiety from medications that had my mind spinning.

I always looked forward to unwinding with the Lord. I felt a level of peace as I penned every thought and unraveled each concern to my Savior.

It had been weeks since I started the new chemotherapy treatment. As I wrote with one hand, my fingers ran through my hair with the other. I noticed clumps of my curly locks landing on the pages of my journal.

Before the ink could dry, a few tears landed on the pages too. The words I'd just written to my Lord were smudged. I let out a weary sigh.

God, please let this all be worthwhile in the end.

I didn't realize I was in the eye of a storm

A Colorado blessing includes the sun-filled days that occupy the sky in every season, even in the dead of winter. On this unusually gloomy day, the atmosphere seemed to agree with what was getting ready to transpire in my body.

I gazed outside, attuning my ears to the sound of the rain's gentle tapping on my window. I opened the window slightly, enough so the earthly scent could pour inside, without wetting the cushions that sat beneath it.

Dark clouds moved almost undetected as they covered the horizon. The rain picked up fervor with each passing moment. Its gentle tapping was now a solid thumping. Closing my eyes, I allowed its rhythm to soothe my soul.

I was unaware that I, too, was about to be submerged within the rainstorm the progression of kidney disease would rumble into my life.

I wasn't the only one caught in the downpour.

Ben's persistence and superhero ways

Ben paced the room.

We recently got married, and he never failed to keep a close eye on me since we began dating—even more so once we said, "I do."

He watched as I struggled to muster enough energy to stand from the cushy oversized chair I had plunged into hours earlier. With every ounce of vitality sucked from me, all I wanted to do was sleep.

He pleaded with me to do otherwise.

"Mimi, you can't sleep now; something's wrong. Let's go to the hospital."

"No, Benny, please, I just need a nap."

I could read his thoughts as he tenderly reached over and caressed my face.

If she falls asleep, she may never wake up.

I eased into the musical nature of the rain as I focused on its pinging. I felt a weightiness consume my body, inviting me to cozy up with a blanket and rest a while.

Ben remained concerned and urged me to let him take me to the hospital. I dozed off, and before I knew it, He swooped me up in his arms and was carrying me to the car. There was no time to grab his cape on the way.

I guess I was going to the hospital, whether I wanted to or not. His insistence saved my life.

An emergency room visit we would never forget

Over the years, chronic illness bullied me in and out of emergency rooms, more than I care to recall, often resulting in short hospital stays. This ER visit was the pinnacle of them all, with life-altering news. It was followed by a six-week stay in the hospital.

Everything seemed a blur, but I was still aware of the constant barrage of busyness all around me. Automatic sliding doors incessantly opened and closed. I noticed a robust man with labored breathing who joined me in the waiting room. His doting wife held him close with one arm and clutched her purse tightly in her lap with the other.

On my left, a mother cradled her limp child who on a normal day would likely be running the halls with careless joy. I could smell the coffee coming from the paper cup she nervously sipped from to keep herself from nodding off. I knew exactly how she felt and kept myself awake by fiddling with the plastic ER admittance bracelet around my wrist.

At last, I was called in.

They drew my blood, and lab work was ordered. I fell asleep while waiting for the results.

My snooze was interrupted by the clanging of items being placed on sterile metal trays and the swoosh of dividing curtains being flung back and forth.

I awoke to see Ben's watery crystal-blue eyes leaning over the metal guardrail that encased my hospital bed. He received the news first.

After a full year of chemo treatments, my kidneys wouldn't be spared.

The octopus had won.

I was in complete kidney failure.

His elbows were draped over the bars as his hands cradled his chin. Without a single spoken word, I could feel his deep yearning and sadness all rolled up in one. It was emanating from his heart to mine.

Silently, he was asking me to fight.

The doctors gave me a choice. I didn't have to begin dialysis. I was in agony and had been through so much already; the thought of being in the arms of my Savior had a strong pull on my soul.

Along with Ben's sorrow, I pictured my twelve-year-old son. Thoughts about the effect it would have on Nathan to lose his mom beckoned me to rise up.

My decision was made.

Heart Connection

1. Read the lyrics to "Rise Up (Lazarus)" – CAIN.[1] I've provided a link for you here: https://zionlyrics.com/cain-rise-up-lazarus-lyrics.

    Are any phrases resonating with you? If so, ask the Holy Spirit what He wants to communicate to you. In a journal, jot down what you hear.

2. Listen to the song "Rise Up (Lazarus)."[2] I've provided a YouTube link for you here: https://youtu.be/pw8IgPHRBr4.

    What else is the Holy Spirit speaking to your heart? Be sure to write it down.

3. Have there been situations in your life that caused you to have to rise up to an unexpected challenge? Did you question God's faithfulness?

    Ask the Holy Spirit to reveal how God was at work in your life at the time.

4. During hard seasons in life, what did you find helped you get through? Give God thanks for His provision.

5. Have you relied on a promise from the Word of God for a situation in your life, either past or present? If so, write it down and meditate on it.

    Psalm 23:1 says, "The LORD is my shepherd, I lack nothing." The entire Psalm is well-known and speaks of God's comfort and provision. Read it now and ask the Holy Spirit to settle your heart as you do.

Chapter 5

Kidney Failure & Dialysis

I could smell the blood.

I woke up attached to a huge stainless-steel machine. It reminded me of the new refrigerator we purchased, only weeks earlier, for our first home.

I was intimidated by its size, and the fact that I could see my own blood make its way from a clear tube inserted in my chest directly into it didn't help.

I lay there bewildered at this new and unwanted extension of my body.

I found out end-stage renal failure meant I'd no longer be able to urinate. Waste accumulation in the blood disturbs the balance of fluid in our bodies. My kidneys, once responsible for naturally filtering out poisonous body waste and regulating fluid and electrolyte balance, were now rendered useless.[1]

They were unable to perform what they naturally did before, including secreting the hormone that assists with red blood cell production. Out of control blood pressure was the result.

All these essential functions to life, once driven by healthy kidneys, were given over to hemodialysis. This fridge look-alike, and the filtration process it offered, was something I would grow to become all too familiar with—as undesirable as it was to every part of my soul.

"Benny, I look like a monster!"

I shrugged my shoulder up to wipe my tears on the hospital gown. I felt captive to the unsightly tubes sticking out of my chest.

He fastened his eyes to mine with the look I'd grown to know so well over the past five years. The same one that assured me I was his girl no matter what.

He was unfazed by how I thought I looked. Yet, written on his face with every tender half-smile, I sensed that he, too, wasn't undaunted by the uncertain road we were forced to travel ahead.

One thing was clear, rain or shine, we would navigate through it together.

My first day at the dialysis center

I heard Ben shuffling for his car keys in his pocket.

"Let's do this, sweets!"

I think he ramped up his enthusiasm, hoping it would help mine.

I reluctantly put on my shoes and rallied myself by entertaining encouraging thoughts and a quick conversation with God.

At least I can soak in the Word and have some quiet time.

I ended with a bit of sarcasm: *Four hours to be exact, three times a week—every week.*

A reminder came from above to which I replied with a giggle.

Oh, right, and the whole being able to live thing.

The lobby displayed gruesome images of unmanaged diabetes. Foot ulcers and even amputation can occur when diabetics fail to monitor diet and insulin closely.[2] Since diabetes is one of the leading causes of kidney failure, I understood why the photos were there but it wasn't the first thing I wanted to see walking into my first hemodialysis treatment.

I was discouraged enough.

I could smell death all around me as the dialysis nurse led me to weigh in on a massive scale like an animal at a meat market.

Stoic from her own daily grind, she informed me, "We'll chart your weight every time you come in. We have to keep track of the amount of fluid in your body."

My gaze fell to my Nike shoes as I stepped on the scale. The weakness I felt in my body caused me to wonder if I'd get to use them for their intended purpose.

Will I run again?

Are my days of teaching group fitness classes over?

I scanned the room, noticing every chair was occupied with seniors. Tugging on the yoga pants that were already beginning to drape on my diminishing frame, I slumped down in the steel-blue recliner next to my assigned dialysis machine.

Typically, I'd strike up a conversation with anyone at arm's length. Not today, my mouth was sealed frozen.

I don't belong here. No one does.

I thought about how, this time, the smell of blood wasn't just my own. Resisting the urge to cry, a massive lump formed in my throat, making it painful to swallow.

I'm so glad I wore a hat.

I tried covering my puffy eyes beneath it. I didn't want anyone to see the anguish I knew was written all over my face. Tigger was a nickname I'd acquired over the years, but at this moment, the last thing I felt was bouncy.

The administrative team was sensitive to my emotional state and intentionally left completing paperwork until next time. I'm glad they did; I could only take so much.

Viewing dialysis as a blessing

I did poorly on hemodialysis. The filtration process proved to be rigorous for my body, and I dreaded every minute. I was constantly tired and had to fight through headaches and nausea every time I went.

To my right sat a man with salt-and-pepper hair, taking a midmorning snooze. It wasn't uncommon to see sleeping patients, even with blood pressure cuffs pulsating on their arms and the perpetual sound of machines beeping.

I, for one, couldn't sleep. I sat still, hoping it would help the headache and nausea. Tucking my chin under and closing my eyes, I told the nurse, "I think I might throw up."

I had already tried all the available medications for relief, without success. She squeezed my shoulder tenderly, acknowledging my discomfort, and went on to attend to my other neighbor.

I watched as our shared nurse began setting up her dialysis machine. A perfectly manicured silver-haired woman with brightly colored lips sat to my left. Her signature red lipstick advertised the yellow tinge of her teeth all the more. She wore a chiffon scarf around her neck, and I watched as she adjusted the brooch adorning it.

Before she sat down, I noticed her light brown eyes; similar to mine, but hers were surrounded by deep lines she attempted to hide with copious amounts of makeup. Looking at her, I was suddenly reminded of my goal to be a future glam-ma and how miraculous it was that dialysis was offering an avenue for me to get there.

Before 1943, dialysis wasn't an option.[3] That's when Dutch physician Willem Kolff invented the first dialysis machine.[4] The first recorded and successful treatment of one of his patients marked the beginning of kidney failure no longer being the swift death sentence it once was.

I needed to remember, dialysis was a gift, even with all its challenges.

Going from hemodialysis to dialysis at home

After three months of demanding hemodialysis treatments, I was thrilled to hear about another type of filtering I could try, potentially offering fewer side effects. My own abdominal lining, also known as the peritoneum, would be used to filter out waste from my blood.[5]

The first step was the surgical placement of a catheter on the lower part of my abdomen, below my belly button. I would have surgery, placing a plastic tube and connecting piece to my body so that I could hook up to a cycler machine for dialysis.

At this point in my journey, I was no longer the naive nineteen-year-old diagnosed with lupus. I was a well-seasoned patient who had learned to become her own advocate, questioning any and every medication or procedure I was asked to undergo. I decided to do some homework regarding catheters.

I leaned closer to my computer screen, wide-eyed.

Why didn't the surgeon tell me about this option?

Researching catheter placement, I discovered a presternal catheter was successfully used in the 1990s at the University of

Missouri by Dr. Zbylut Twardowski and his colleagues.[6] It allowed the exit site of the plastic tubing and its connecting piece, which attached to the cycler machine, to be located in the chest area rather than the abdomen.

The piece that connected to the machine was rather large for someone my size. It was about the length of a deck of cards and as wide as a Sharpie marker. If placed in my abdominal area, a large bulge would be clearly visible.

Excited about another option, I told Ben all about it.

"Sweetie, if the surgeon lets me do this, I can tuck the tubing and connector piece in my bra, and no one will see it!"

I'm also a bath lover. With the catheter's placement on my upper chest, just below my shoulder, I'd still be able to soak in a tub as long as I didn't submerge the catheter in water. It would be a breeding ground for infection if I did.

The chest area is less germy and doesn't move as freely as abdominal skin, so a presternal catheter is a good option for children as well as obese patients. I didn't fit into the criteria but was hopeful the surgeon would consider it for me anyway.

This type of catheter requires a more challenging surgery and isn't as commonly performed. It's probably the reason my doctor didn't suggest it initially.

The surgeon was willing to try it on me, and after a successful surgery, preparations were made for educating us on peritoneal dialysis.

We learned how to keep me alive—from home!

I took meticulous notes.

Fidgeting incessantly with the pen, I asked the nurse, "What if I screw it up?"

Ben sat rigid in his chair, just as eager for her reply.

"There will be a nurse available twenty-four hours a day. The phone number will be on your machine."

Uncomforted by her reply and keenly aware that taking this information in was critical to my existence, we listened carefully to every word.

She informed us that dialysis would take place at night over a ten-hour period.

A gaping trench, whittled by concerned thoughts, took form in the playground of my mind.

What if the machine breaks?

What if the phone nurse falls asleep?

What if I forget how to do all of this?

The idea of being in the comfort of my own home while receiving treatment was worth the apprehension both Ben and I shared.

Additionally, I might feel better since daily treatments, instead of three times a week with hemodialysis, allowed for less waste and toxins to build up in my blood.

We got hands-on experience with practice sessions at the clinic before trying it by ourselves at home. We first learned a manual method in case something really did happen to the machine. We then moved on to learning all the ins and outs of the cycler.

There was roughly a thirty-minute daily setup and teardown process that seemed complicated, especially at first. Two-minute-long handwashing sessions were the norm before I could touch my catheter.

I'd then connect it to a large bag of dialysate fluid on the cycler machine so that it could travel through my abdominal cavity.

A dwelling period with dialysate solution in my belly allowed for the absorption of toxins before draining them out, along with any excess fluid.[7]

It was an adjustment doing this at home, but a welcomed one. I slept with earplugs because even though the nurse said the machine was quiet, she clearly never listened to it in a silent room in the middle of the night!

In the morning, the exchanges created a waste bag that Ben dumped out into our bathtub. It didn't have handles and was heavy. Not for Ben, but it was for me.

It wasn't the only taxing duty peritoneal dialysis imposed.

Enter my hero, Ben, yet again!

Settling into a routine with new norms

I tapped the phone symbol on my smartphone. Instantly, my favorite's list appeared with my favorite person answering on the other end.

"Benny, the bags are here again. There's like twenty boxes this time."

"Don't worry, sugar; I'll be home soon."

Delivery of the dialysate fluid only came every two weeks or so. Each box weighed in at about twenty-six pounds and housed only two bags, enough for one day. They weren't exactly my idea of desirable living room décor, so Ben brought them down to our basement every time the shipment came in. He stacked them underneath our stairs, taking up the entire storage area.

He never complained, not once.

I wondered how the elderly, on home dialysis, accomplished the task of putting the bags on the machine by themselves, let alone organizing the boxes in a less conspicuous space. Maybe that's why I noticed so many seniors at the hemodialysis center?

I was thankful for Ben's help and told him so every night. As the weeks progressed, we had an efficient system underway. By the time I finished sanitizing my hands, Ben arrived with my nightly supply of dialysate fluid from the basement. He placed it on the cycler, which took up every inch of my nightstand.

"Aren't you glad you gave home dialysis a try? You seem so much better." He sat on the bed, dismantling the box the solution came in while listening for my reply.

"Oh my gosh, honey, I'm not nauseous anymore, and I actually have energy again!"

Six weeks after the catheter placement, and with several weeks of peritoneal dialysis under my belt, I was back to teaching my weekly spin class!

Renal failure dietary guidelines threw me for a loop

Dialysis, either hemodialysis or peritoneal, can only partially compensate for the loss of natural kidney function. Since not all toxins are removed, extra guanidine and polyamine remained in my blood and contributed to a lack of appetite.[8] Turns out, not being hungry was a blessing in disguise since I was under a highly restrictive diet from here on out.

I always emphasized the importance of nutrient-dense food, both for myself and my clients. The prescribed dialysis diet was the polar opposite of how I was used to eating and what I recommended to others for optimal health.

Everything I'd learned about nutrition professionally had to be set to the wayside when it came to what I put in my mouth. This new way of eating was something I needed to get on board with. If I didn't, it could produce life-threatening consequences.

Phosphorus

I was told to keep my protein levels up but limit phosphorus[9]—a catch-22. As a nutrition guide, I knew foods like eggs, meat, poultry, fish, nuts, and seeds pack a huge protein punch. They also contain large amounts of the mineral I was supposed to avoid.

Reducing these foods, and even eliminating some of them, was required. Doing so would help ease muscle aches and pains, itching, and most imperatively, keep calcifications in bones and blood vessels from forming.[10]

After a few weeks on dialysis, I ended up in the hospital for a short stint with dangerously high phosphorus levels.

I could hear the shifting of pills as the nurse handed me the large bottle. She explained, "These are phosphate binders. Take them at every meal to keep your phosphorus levels down."

My eyes widened after opening it, "Oh my gosh, these are horse pills! How am I supposed to swallow them?"

Unfortunately, their size wasn't indicative of their value as far as being able to do the job fully. My levels were consistently high, even though I complied with all the new diet rules I was asked to follow.

Did I mention drinking coffee was out too?

Potassium

Coffee has large amounts of potassium. I was told to avoid even the smallest amount.

Too much or too little potassium posed its own set of problems. The body needs the right amount of potassium for nerve and muscle cells to function properly. A potassium deficiency could lead to digestive disorders, increase the risk of heart disease, stroke, and even cancer.[11]

An abundance causes minor disturbances like nausea, fatigue, and muscle weakness. More troubling was the potential for breathing issues, disrupted heartbeat, seizures, paralysis, and coma.[12]

As with phosphorus, my labs always leaned toward elevated levels. To remedy the situation, I was also told to avoid fruits and vegetables.[13]

I had a hard time grasping it all; the very foods I was accustomed to eating, the ones I knew promoted health and wellness, were to be severely limited!

I was essentially on a two-year-old's dream diet of white flour and sugar—two recommended staples.

Bring on the rainbow Skittles, I guess?

Sodium

Sodium was also under scrutiny to help keep fluid balance and blood pressure in check.[14] I was told to shoot for 1200 mg or less of sodium a day.

Foods like soups, lunch meats, and cheese were clearly not invited on my plate, but some sneakier culprits were also banned. Bread, cereals, and chicken are surprisingly stacked with sodium too.[15]

A piece of packaged uncooked chicken from the supermarket already has large amounts of salt, without the customary sprinkle from a saltshaker. Poultry is often injected with a mix of water, salt, and other additives to make the meat juicier and more tender.[16] A four-ounce serving of chicken contained more than a third of my daily allotment!

Eliminating sodium from my diet caused my newly sensitive taste buds to become experts at detecting it. They would prove, time and again, eating out was the biggest source of all, with elevated blood pressure confirming it.

My nutrient-deprived body deteriorated over time

The dialysis diet felt impossible to comply with, but I still followed the recommendations as closely as possible. The diet may have kept the unwanted side effects of unbalanced phosphorous, potassium, and sodium levels, but did nothing as far as giving me any sort of vitality or energy for my already weak and deteriorating body.

My aversion to swallowing the oversized phosphate binders and lack of appetite certainly didn't help matters either. A diet void of nutrition, coupled with stubborn toxins that eventually refused the dialysis process, was detrimental.

Even with all the wellness knowledge I had, I couldn't do a single thing about it. I was up to sixteen hours of peritoneal dialysis daily. We were facing a stark reality: dialysis was no longer cutting it.

I was slowly dying.

Heart Connection

1. Read the lyrics to "Oceans (Where Feet May Fail)" – Hillsong UNITED.[17] I've provided a link for you here: https://www.azlyrics.com/lyrics/hillsongunited/oceanswherefeetmayfail.html.

   Are any phrases resonating with you? If so, ask the Holy Spirit what He wants to communicate to you. In a journal, jot down what you hear.

2. Listen to the song "Oceans (Where Feet May Fail)."[18] I've provided a YouTube link for you here: https://youtu.be/dy9nwe9_xzw.

   What else is the Holy Spirit speaking to your heart? Be sure to write it down.

3. I have to admit, I feel a bit uneasy when I read and hear the lyric, "Spirit lead me where my trust is without borders." It feels comforting when I have a sense of control over my circumstances, but that's not always the case.

   Talk to the Holy Spirit about what you can do when you find yourself feeling vulnerable or powerless.

4. What situations are you currently facing that lead you to a place of complete trust in someone or something outside of yourself?

   Ask the Holy Spirit what you can do to help alleviate any stress associated with that.

5. Is there a situation in your life that seemingly has no solution?

   If so, ask the Holy Spirit to comfort you and guide you toward hope. What is He speaking to you? Be sure to write it down and refer back to it when you come into a place of concern over your situation.

Chapter 6

A Plea for Life Answered

I was given a death sentence.

Doctors told me that without a kidney transplant, I had about a year to live. When I began dialysis, I was placed on the National Kidney Registry and was told the typical wait for a kidney was three to five years.[1]

My nephrologist advised, "It's wise to seek out a live donor."

Dr. S. continued, "Is there someone you know that's willing to be tested? Perhaps a family member or friend?"

Their blood would have to play well with mine, and the testing process was rather lengthy, but those weren't the biggest obstacles.

How in the world was I going to ask someone to give me one of their organs? Asking for a ride to a doctor's appointment when I couldn't drive myself was challenging enough! For someone like me, who didn't feel worthy enough to ask for help, I had an aversion to burdening others.

This wasn't just a favor. This was big time! I couldn't even fathom approaching the subject. What was I supposed to say?

"Spare kidney, anyone?"

A plea for life was answered through social media

Ultimately, that's exactly what happened. My mother-in-law got the ball rolling and made a plea through Facebook. Ben's brother framed a picture of me with the caption, "Dat smile, needs a kidney," and they both tagged me in their posts.

Soon, responses came in from people I hadn't heard from in years, including past workmates and friends from high school.

Social media certainly has its negatives—one of them being getting mindlessly sucked in, scrolling for hours while dishes and laundry pile up. In this case, social media was actually productive. So many selfless people responded.

In fact, there was such a huge response that the transplant hospital was inundated with phone calls. I'll never forget when, Armie, one of the kidney transplant administrators called.

"Mrs. Kroger, we aren't able to handle all the donation inquiries on your behalf."

Apparently, God had deployed His own army to come to my rescue.

I couldn't believe it.

An unexpected phone call crushing all hope

I sat on the stairs, too exhausted and nauseated to make the flight up. I felt a customary headache coming on also. Hemodialysis side effects were taking charge of my body once again.

I slouched on the bottom step, deciding whether or not to take my shoes off before climbing up the stairs. That's when I heard my cell phone ring.

I rummaged through my purse that was still slung over my shoulder. It took all I had to find my phone and lift it to my ear.

I answered with a frail whisper, "Hello?"

It was a friend who had responded to my mother-in-law's Facebook post about donating a kidney. She was months into the testing process on my behalf.

Testing for kidney donation is an arduous process, taking a minimum of three months, but often six, depending on how quickly the donor meets all the requirements. It's about far more than physiological compatibility.[2] A medical history review and exam is the first step, followed by a gamut of others.

A financial consultation is next. A recipient's insurance will often cover medical expenses for themselves as well as the donor, but lost wages during the recovery are not included. A potential donor is made aware of how donation might affect them financially and requires their agreement before moving forward.

Immunological and laboratory tests are next on the agenda, including an EKG to assess heart function and a chest X-ray to determine lung health. So much blood is drawn for labs, leaving a donor wondering if they'll have any blood left by the end of it all!

A psychological evaluation is then used to determine a donor's motivation. The transplant administrators want to make sure the donor is willingly donating without pressure. They also want to make sure the donor isn't financially incentivized.

The final step involves urine samples. Female donor candidates also undergo mammograms and gynecological exams.

We were far into the testing process, so I was blindsided when I answered my soon-to-be donor's phone call and heard the news.

She changed her mind—she was withdrawing from any further donation testing.

Giving someone else your *spare* kidney is a tremendous sacrifice, so I completely understood, but it didn't change the letdown and swirl of emotions that gusted in my heart over this turn of events.

Another offer came quickly and renewed my hope

Leif's wife, Vikki, one of my closest friends, knew my current donor candidate had decided to forgo continuing in the testing process.

Leif, also a dear friend, looked at me intently. His eyes narrowed as he studied mine.

"I'm giving you my kidney, Mimi, and I won't change my mind."

He couldn't have said it more resolutely. I felt the pain from the latest disappointment being massaged out of my soul as he spoke. Each word resounded with a steady conviction that would turn the biggest skeptic into a believer.

I was usually the latter, but I had experienced a blow to hope that would leave even the colossal optimist in a deep pit of angst.

Leif tossed the rope down and drew me from the pit of despair after my fall. A rescue like this was not uncommon to a man of his caliber—he was a firefighter by trade.

When Leif initially discussed with Vikki his conviction to donate, she struggled briefly with his desire to come to the rescue. In light of what they had recently experienced in their own lives, I understood why.

This resilient and God-held couple have their own story that is theirs alone to tell. However, I would be remiss if I didn't mention that they had an unfathomable loss only weeks prior to Leif's decision to offer me his gift of life.

Their one-of-a-kind, sparkly two-and-a-half-year-old daughter, Carli, passed away suddenly. The spitting image of Leif, she lit up a room and any mood with a mere glance of her shimmering crystal-blue eyes and sweet-as-apple-pie smile.

She was love in its purest form. Even her wispy blonde hair was indicative of how she could breeze into a room, take any tinge of darkness, and whirl it to flight with the tiny flick of a platinum strand in your direction.

Vikki's apprehension was more than warranted. The thought of another loss would have anyone questioning the risk, let alone someone who had just been dealt the most devastating blow to a mother's soul.

Leif, equally wrenched with the same suffering, turned his attention to giving the very thing his own family had been recently deprived of: life. The risks associated with donation didn't deter him one bit, and both he and Vikki decided they would give in honor of their ladybug, Carli.

Donation risks and the many willing to give

Have you ever watched a commercial on television giving you all the side effects of a medication they're advertising? You listen to the worst of the worst, often including the possibility of death, all the while watching a person on a scenic bike ride enjoying life without a care in the world. As rare as complications may be, the question to ponder is always, do the benefits outweigh the risks?

In general, kidney donation has minimal long-term effects, but any major surgery poses potential complications. Leif was willing to risk pain, infection, pneumonia, blood clotting, urinary tract infection, allergic reaction to anesthesia, a collapsed lung, and yes, even death, all to benefit me.[3] Others were willing to risk it all too.

Ben's cousin Jamie, a lively and sweet blonde beauty who lives in Minnesota, was also willing to donate. She was one of the top three in the running. With obviously fewer hurdles to jump through, a local donor was a more feasible candidate, but she still went far in the testing process. If she had been the only viable option, she likely would have been chosen.

Who knows, maybe with her kidney inside my body, I might have had the opportunity to discover if blondes really do have more fun. I would still get to test that theory with Leif's kidney. Unless, of course, it only applies to females.

Mandi, my friend and personal training client, was also under serious consideration and made several trips to the transplant hospital to undergo approval. She was testing for donation right alongside Jamie and Leif. If willpower was the only determining factor, Mandi would have won.

Shaking her head and snapping her fingers at the defeat, she told me, "I only had one more urine sample to go when Leif beat me to the punch."

Mandi gets her admirable grit from her father who owns an ambulance company in a small Colorado town. I imagine, having ridden along with her dad on rescue calls after school while doing homework in the passenger seat, there wasn't much this spunky little girl hadn't seen.

Today, Mandi is the type of person who is also a first responder, getting things done with tenacity and strength. When there's no one around to help, well, she'll just do it herself!

It's no surprise she still says these very words to me today, without hesitation, "My kidney is yours if you ever need another one."

I'm amazed at the treasure of people willing to give in this tremendous way. I couldn't possibly mention every person who made an effort to donate. For each person who did, thank you! You're a healing gift to my heart. You know who you are, and so do I. I smile from ear to ear in thinking of you and always will.

A new kidney and healing in more ways than one

With a year fast approaching since my first dialysis treatment, death was knocking on my door. I like to say, "The Lord came through at the eleventh hour." Eleven months in, I received a healthy, new-to-me kidney from my friend Leif.

My transplant was seven years ago, and my new kidney is an absolute rock star! My labs are better than a young person with two healthy kidneys, and I couldn't be more grateful.

I've had the honor of being on the receiving end of an ultimate sacrifice. Someone willing to risk their life for mine is a beyond words, incredible gift. I don't have the ability to fully express how grateful I am!

In the Bible, God touches on the magnitude of love that comes in doing what Leif did for me. "Greater love has no one than this, that someone lay down his life for his friends" (John 15:13 ESV). Jesus did the same for all humanity.

That's how valuable we are to him!

Up to this point, I'd been familiar with the love of Jesus and was learning He was faithful in caring for me, but honestly, I wasn't sure people loved me—at least not unconditionally.

It wasn't until Leif's sacrificial act of kindness, through his willingness to rescue me from death, when I began to realize I was loved and could trust people. Even before then, the revelation came as I watched, time and again, people coming through for me without a single string attached.

The doctors, nurses, and staff I've worked with have blessed me with their valuable time and genuine care over the years. Dr. Schlessinger is a stellar physician, and I'm grateful for Dr. Wiseman and the entire kidney clinic team at the University of Colorado Anschutz Medical Campus. A special thanks to Dr. Igal Kam, my skilled transplant surgeon.

I even made a few friends along the way, including a caring nurse named Randy, who made me feel special and at home during one of my extended stays at the hospital. My friend James stands out too. He worked in the housekeeping department and kept me company on occasion, with conversations about the Savior we shared.

Everyone willing to be tested for kidney donation spoke volumes to my soul. Also, friends like Steph, who of her own accord, researched how I was to take care of myself during dialysis.

All the prayers that went up on my behalf were priceless. When I wasn't able to work, our generous church contributed financially. People in our church family sent grocery gift cards and provided meals, with no expectation of even getting their Tupperware back.

My soul continued to soar with the countless cards, messages, and gifts from friends and family. The people in my life who accompanied me to doctor's visits or sat with me during chemotherapy or dreaded hemodialysis treatments likely didn't realize the heart restoration they were a part of.

They all helped to heal parts of my soul I never knew needed healing.

All of these unconditional acts of kindness began a process of unraveling the lies I once believed about myself and others.

I now understood I had value, I was loved, and people could be trusted.

Those truths, along with many others, brought wholeness to my soul, which culminated in a healthy body too.

I haven't dealt with the octopus since.

God's victory is sure and there's purpose for the pain

Life's hurts can create belief systems, keeping us from understanding our worth and trusting others with our hearts.

There's a healing of the soul that can affect how we're doing physically. It isn't always the situation, but that truth was undeniable for me.

We've all experienced pain, but I can assure you God catches every tear and makes a treasure out of each one. Psalm 56:8 (NLT) tells us, "You keep track of all my sorrows. You have collected all my tears in your bottle. You have recorded each one in your book."

Don't get me wrong, God didn't author sickness in my life. That's the sole job description of the enemy. I do believe, however, God made use of what the devil attempted to harm me with.

Joseph, from the Bible, experienced the same. Genesis 50:20 says, "You intended to harm me, but God intended it for good to accomplish what is now being done, the saving of many lives."

God is on our side through every battle, and we can rest assured, the devil never wins. The enemy thought he had the victory when Jesus went to the cross. He plotted for Jesus' death, and it ended up being what brought salvation to the entire world!

The very thing the enemy tried to use to take me out, God used to usher me into the fullness of what He created me for. He brought transformation through it, using it to establish my identity as a highly valued daughter of the King.

I want that for you too!

My healing process began at salvation when I learned God unconditionally loved me. He proved it on the cross when He took every one of my sins. He continued to show me His love when He provided for my every need during my life's journey and topped it off with a transformed life full of purpose.

God was big enough to use all I went through for my profit and for the benefit of others. As I share my story, it has the ability to bring others into a place of health and wholeness too.

He imparted an assurance that He has a plan for my life and that it's important to Him that I walk in it. He designed me for something specific—a call, a destiny, a life with meaning.

I'm still here for a reason, and so are you!

Turning to the One who heals us

Our freedom depends on our ability to turn from self-reliance and to the only One who can heal and fully cleanse us from sin and shame. He reveals to us what's really going on in our hearts through the guidance and counsel of the Holy Spirit.

Isaiah 48:17 says, "This is what the LORD says—your Redeemer, the Holy One of Israel: 'I am the LORD your God, who teaches you what is best for you, who directs you in the way you should go.'"

There isn't a one-size-fits-all approach with God; He is too personal for that. But I believe He will use the insights I was given to help lead you into your own promised land—free from disease and dysfunction.

God will give you your own personal strategy through intimacy with Him. My prayer is that you'll experience the power of a loving God who never fails. The One who is called Healer. His name is Jesus, and the avenue to hear from Him is the Holy Spirit.

First things first, let's see how we connect with God so you can come away with your own heart revelations that will bring healing to your soul and body.

Heart Connection

1. Read the lyrics to "Scars" – I AM THEY.[4] I've provided a link for you here: https://www.azlyrics.com/lyrics/iamthey/scars.html.

   Are any phrases resonating with you? If so, ask the Holy Spirit what He wants to communicate to you. In a journal, jot down what you hear.

2. Listen to the song "Scars."[5] I've provided a YouTube link for you here: https://youtu.be/OqjGT9BSyJA.

   What else is the Holy Spirit speaking to your heart? Be sure to write it down.

3. Has there been a gift you've received in your life that changed you? What was it? It could be a person or a meaningful gift given to you at just the right time. The Bible says in James 1:17, "Every good and perfect gift is from above, coming down from the Father of the heavenly lights, who does not change like shifting shadows."

   Write a letter to God, thanking Him for the gift and His faithfulness.

4. Have you given someone a gift lately? One of the most uplifting things we can do is give our time or resources to benefit someone else. How can you cultivate being a giver?

   Ask the Holy Spirit what you can do to bless someone today.

5. What have you learned through some of your biggest life challenges? Think about how they have affected you, both positively and negatively.

   Ask the Holy Spirit to help you to focus on the positive. Allow Him to direct you to what you gained from your experience.

Part 2
Prospering in Spirit

Chapter 7

Opening Communication with God

Enlightenment and freedom from ailments—whether in our souls or our physical bodies—comes from the most neglected Person in the church.

His name is Holy Spirit.

He is very often overlooked. That's not a surprise, since the enemy loves nothing more than to block communication with our Creator. The One who made you, He alone knows how to fix everything in you that's causing pain, and it's His pleasure to do it.

The Holy Spirit enables us to perceive and understand that which leads to life and away from death. Death is anything that keeps us from the abundant life God wants us to enjoy. Unrest in spirit, soul, or body leads to decay and death.

The active Presence of the Holy Spirit in our lives is where our power out of death and into life comes from. Integration with Him is what allows permanent transformation and healing. Reading *about* God in the Bible isn't enough. Not when the enemy of our soul is always ready to attack us on every front.

1 Peter 5:8 says, "Be alert and of sober mind. Your enemy the devil prowls around *like* a roaring lion looking for someone to devour." Make no mistake; he is no lion. He only comes acting like one, but his bite can be vicious nonetheless—especially if we lack the voice of God in our lives.

As we cultivate intimacy with the Holy Spirit, we are able to hear from God. He becomes our defense against the lies and attacks of the enemy.

First, let's build the foundation that allows for communication with God. It's imperative for our survival and ultimate healing as we navigate through life. Jesus says in John 16:33b-d, "In this world you will have trouble. But take heart! I have overcome the world."

Opening the lines of communication

Like it or not, we're in a war. Our enemy's defeat is sure, but we must listen for truth and direction from the Holy Spirit. We need help from someone who is unequivocally on our side; we need the voice of God Himself.

Wikipedia defines a *line of communication* as "the route that connects an operating military unit with its supply base."[1] It goes on to say, "Supplies and reinforcements are transported along the line of communication. Therefore, a secure and open line of communication is vital for any military force to continue to operate effectively."

A person without an open line of communication with the Father is vulnerable to defeat through isolation. This person lacks the ability to ask for reinforcements and supply. However, reservoirs of resources are available for those who seek the face of God and listen for His voice. The conduit by which we can hear from Him is the Holy Spirit.

The ability to oppose enemy forces is directly related to our access to Heaven's headquarters at all times. Philippians 4:19 assures us, "And my God will meet all your needs according to the riches of his glory in Christ Jesus." Our chief commanding officer is Jesus—through the indwelling Presence of the Holy Spirit.

To gain access to the Holy Spirit, we must first believe by faith in the work Christ did through the cross and His resurrection. Every single person on this side of Heaven has an invitation from God to receive the priceless gift of open communication with Him through the saving work of Christ.

God makes a way for relationship with Him

God's ultimate act of love was in rescuing us from sin. That weighty truth has made its way into every football stadium end zone in America. Brightly colored poster boards and cardboard signs dance with the Scripture reference John 3:16.

It says this: "For God so loved the world that he gave his one and only Son, that whoever believes in him shall not perish but have eternal life." This Scripture presents the sturdy foundation on which we rely for eternal salvation and gives us the ability to hear from God today.

In the Old Testament, the people of God were required to give blood sacrifices to cover their sins.[2] This practice brought about the restoration of their relationship with God after disobedience. Hebrews 9:22 tells us, "Without the shedding of blood there is no forgiveness."

This was never God's initial intention, but the fall of Adam and Eve into sin ignited a sacrificial blood system to bring reconciliation. This practice was in place for generations until God provided a permanent solution.

Jesus would later meet every requirement for reconciliation with God through His own blood. For those who believe, provision was made for the eternal restoration of contact between God and man through Jesus Christ.

The first sin broke communion with the Father

The first-ever sacrifice came after Adam and Eve sinned. They disobeyed God and were ashamed as a result. Realizing they were naked, they became fearful and isolated themselves. They hid from the very One who gave them the bodies that were now cloaked with self-induced shame.

"Then the man and his wife heard the sound of the Lord God as he was walking in the garden in the cool of the day, and *they hid* from the Lord God among the trees of the garden" (Genesis 3:8).

Can you smell the dew on the leaves and hear the dense sound of God's footsteps as He drew near them? One step followed another, leaving its imprint in the moist soil. Adam and Eve scattered in fear. Retreating aimlessly from their Holy Father, seemed to them, a necessary consequence for their disobedience.

Yet God, in His love and mercy, sought them out, "But the Lord God called to the man, 'Where are you?'" (Genesis 3:9). The Father's desire was never to be separated from having a relationship with them, and it remains His heart's cry toward us today.

It all began with a warning. God told Adam in Genesis 2:16–17, "And the Lord God commanded the man, 'You are free to eat from any tree in the garden; but you must not eat from the tree of the knowledge of good and evil, for when you eat from it you will certainly die.'"

We know, as we read beyond this first account of sin in the garden, Adam and Eve did eat from the tree, and yet they continued to live physically. The death God spoke of was a spiritual death. It was death to an eternal connection with their God, who created and loved them.

God's desire in giving the command was only for their protection. He wanted to shield them from the pain that would inevitably follow. In eating the fruit, they awoke within themselves an awareness of evil and its consequences.

In Genesis 3:5, Satan enticed Eve, "For God knows that when you eat from it your eyes will be opened, and you will be like God, knowing good and evil." He made it sound as if God were keeping something from her, when all along, He was sheltering her.

Until that point, Adam and Eve's life experience was only good. "God saw all that he had made, and it was very good" (Genesis 1:31). They went from a life of absolute perfection, with souls experiencing only virtue, and stepped into a world of fear, shame, chaos, and destruction.

I believe the most daunting change must have been the brokenness they felt as their relationship with their Heavenly Creator and Father was now different for them than it had ever been.

He didn't change, but they did.

Sin brought chaos and suffering to the soul of man

The consequence of sin was new to them. Shame, guilt, and fear came rushing in. As a result, God's children withdrew from communing and communicating with their Father. Adam and Eve relinquished freedom from sin.

They buried themselves under shame and condemnation and it was too much for them to bear. Their undisturbed and harmonious relationship with the Father was marred. Loaded with these foreign emotions, they chose to separate themselves from their Creator whose heart always desired for them to run to Him rather than away from Him.

Listening as God asked Adam of his whereabouts, I can picture Adam's chin tucked in close to his chest with ears attuned to his racing heartbeat thumping. His shaking hands clutching the trunk of a tree, perhaps the very one that produced the fruit that enticed Eve, only hours earlier.

With his frame hidden behind its wide trunk, I imagine he strained to quiver the following reply to God when asked about his whereabouts, "He answered, 'I heard you in the garden, and I was afraid because I was naked; so I hid' " (Genesis 3:10).

Would Adam dare come out from behind his hidden shelter and look upon the face of the One who he had betrayed? God saw to it. It went against His nature not to.

He would absolutely come to the rescue of His beloved children.

Their souls were in pieces. They were never intended to experience such tragic emotions. Created in the very image of the One who made them, they were made for love.

Genesis 1:27 tells us, "So God created mankind in his own image, in the image of God he created them; male and female he created them." God molded them like Himself, which meant humans possessed the essential characteristics of the One who made them.

1 John 4:8 tells us, "God is love."

When evil entered through sin, a major disturbance rippled through the very essence of who God created man to be. Like Adam and Eve, we are designed to live in a love-infused realm. Enduring experiences that are outside of love affects us in spirit and soul. Often, our physical body also reacts to the disruption.

God is Holy (1 Peter 1:16). Holiness was then a part of Adam and Eve's DNA as well. Sin was contrary to the loving and holy nature they were created to rest in and enjoy.

Discord entered and tore apart the very core of who they were. The disturbance was irreversible, without the redemptive work of their Father.

God stayed the same, "Come to Papa"

Sin changed man, but God remained the same. 2 Timothy 2:13 tells us, "If we are faithless, he remains faithful, for he cannot disown himself." At their rebellion, God was still fully loving and ever holy. Congruent with His indestructible nature, He provided a way out that satisfied both of these attributes and many more. Along with love, His mercy and grace flowed fervently toward them. His passion for them was undeniable and irreversible.

At the beckoning of God, Adam eventually turned to meet the face of God and discovered his Father's steadfast love, despite his own faulty actions. As their eyes met, Adam experienced firsthand the truth from Malachi 3:6 (ESV), "For I the LORD do not change; therefore you, O children of Jacob, are not consumed."

God remained true to His nature of pure love, and because of His unchanging character, He made lavish provision for their pardon.

He broke their self-imposed silence as He sought them out and provided garments for them to cover up. God knew it would, at the least, alleviate the shame they now carried over their nakedness. His changeless love overcame the fear and darkness that gripped them.

In images depicting Adam and Eve, we see fig leaves used as a covering, but that wasn't the case. Genesis 3:21 (NLT) says, "And the LORD God made clothing from *animal skins* for Adam and his wife."

Sin had a price. The life of an innocent animal—one of God's creations—was sacrificed for their disobedience. Blood was spilled, so their nakedness could be covered.

Holiness has two sides, much like a coin. Its face shines holy, and its tail reflects justice. Every aspect of who God is doesn't change. Restitution for sin had to be made to satisfy justice. The blood system for atonement was birthed as a result of this first sin and continued up until Christ.

The man who hung willingly and obediently on a blood-stained cross put an end to it when He said, with His last earthly breath, "It is finished" (John 19:30).

It was God's ultimate provision, and it cost Him His very own flawless Son.

Jesus, as a man, pays the penalty for our sins

Jesus became the spotless Lamb of God who was sacrificed for us. John the Baptist makes the announcement in John 1:29, "The next day John saw Jesus coming toward him and said, 'Look, the Lamb of God, who takes away the sin of the world!' "

Jesus came, as a man, into a world riddled with sin and yet remained unblemished. He chose obedience every time He was faced with temptation. He did it because of His intense love for God's creation, and humbly experienced humanity personally. He willingly came to earth as one of us.

Philippians 2:6–8 (NLT) tells us, "Though he was God, he did not think of equality with God as something to cling to. Instead, he gave up his divine privileges; he took the humble position of a slave and was born as a human being. When he appeared in human form, he humbled himself in obedience to God and died a criminal's death on a cross."

Whoa! I don't know anyone on this side of Heaven who would readily choose to leave Paradise to serve a world that would accuse, reject, and go as far as murdering them.

Isaiah 53:7 tells us, "He was oppressed and afflicted, yet he did not open his mouth; he was led like a lamb to the slaughter, and as a sheep before its shearers is silent, so he did not open his mouth."

Jesus refused to defend His innocence because He knew it would ultimately bring back ours.

What an honor to be the recipient of His altruistic love. Jesus humbly stepped down from the Divine. He went from an atmosphere of purity and glory to become a man with a body like ours. One in which He would be susceptible to temptation, just like you and me. The fact that He never sinned and overcame every temptation common to man qualifies Him to be our Savior.

God provides a way back to Him through Christ

Where we have failed, Christ has remained faithful. In the deepest sense, He is the ultimate scapegoat. His perfection becomes our own as we step into truth and believe He took our place, sacrificing Himself so that we could become righteous in the sight of God.

Romans 5:1 (CEB) confirms, "Therefore, since we have been made righteous through his faithfulness combined with our faith, we have peace with God through our Lord Jesus Christ." This peace allows for open communication with a Holy God who loves us beyond words and provides the way for us to come back into fellowship with Him.

The cross expresses the pinnacle of the Father's love, as Jesus overcomes sin on our behalf. It restores a connection with our Heavenly Father, as our sins are blotted out. Psalm 103:12 exhorts us, "As far as the east is from the west, so far has he removed our transgressions from us."

All Jesus suffered for us was enough not just to cover sin, but to completely obliterate it from God's sight. Hebrews 8:12 explains, "For I will forgive their wickedness and will remember their sins no more."

What we've been unable to do in resisting temptation, Jesus does for us. 1 Peter 2:24 says, " 'He himself bore our sins' in his body on the cross, so that we might die to sins and live for righteousness; 'by his wounds you have been healed.' "

A provision for life and healing comes through Christ's redemptive work. It brings us back into sweet communion with a Father who possesses an irrefutable loving nature toward us. It is simply who He is. Sin itself lacks the power to change God's loving nature. He will always be true to Himself, and that means He remains true to us.

Inheritance through Adam and Eve brought death

We inherited from our human ancestors, Adam and Eve, a sinful nature. A propensity to sin was passed on to us. David writes about it in Psalm 51:5 (ESV), "Behold, I was brought forth in iniquity, and in sin did my mother conceive me."

That doesn't seem very fair, does it? After all, we didn't eat the fruit! All pride begins to trickle down as we consider the likelihood of ourselves making the same decision they did if placed in the same scenario. Ego makes its final tumble when we think about how unfair it is that an innocent man, God the Son, chooses to redeem us from the consequence of their act of rebellion—as well as our own.

Romans 5:17 tells of our great gain in Christ, "For if, by the trespass of the one man, death reigned through that one man, how much more will those who receive God's abundant provision of grace and of the gift of righteousness reign in life through the one man, Jesus Christ!" The spiritual death stemming from that first sinful bite—which was passed on to us—is overthrown by God's incredible mercy and grace through His Son and our Savior.

Jesus knew the fallen nature of man and that without His atoning sacrifice, it was impossible for us to overcome sin and triumph on our own. Hebrews 4:15 refers to Jesus in saying, "For we do not have a high priest who is unable to empathize with our weaknesses, but we have one who has been tempted in every way, just as we are—yet he did not sin."

The final inheritance through Christ brings life

The Savior overcame giving in to sin and took hold of redeeming for us what Adam and Eve had so foolishly given away. Jesus felt the effect of resisting sin to the greatest degree because He went to the furthest point of temptation, and further still since He never sinned.

You and I can't say the same. Out of sheer personal experience, we don't need much convincing on this point, but Romans 3:23 (NLT) reminds us, "For everyone has sinned; we all fall short of God's glorious standard."

We need a Savior!

The reality is that on our own, we don't have the capacity to free ourselves from sin. Thankfully, God doesn't leave us in defeat. Romans 3:24 (NLT) continues, "Yet God, in his grace, freely makes us right in his sight. He did this through Christ Jesus when he freed us from the penalty for our sins."

A tremendous gift is offered to anyone who chooses to put their faith in Jesus' atoning work for them by way of the cross. Our part is to believe, and even that is a gift from God. Ephesians 2:8–9 says, "For it is by grace you have been saved, through faith—and this is not from yourselves, it is the gift of God—not by works, so that no one can boast."

It shouldn't be surprising then that a Christian is called a "believer," and it's no wonder the Gospel is called The Good News.

Receiving freely without deserving it truly is good news!

Communication with God is a gift you can receive

If you haven't already accepted the gift of Christ Jesus, here's your chance! It's really easy to do. Romans 10:9 tells us, "If you declare with your mouth, 'Jesus is Lord,' and believe in your heart that God raised him from the dead, you will be saved."

Are you ready to declare with me? You're welcome to speak to God and accept all He has for you in your own words. But if you'd like some help, pray this:

Father God, I've sinned. I ask you to forgive me. I look to Jesus as my Redeemer, my Savior, and Lord. I thank you for making a way for me to be righteous through the blood of Christ, shed for me. I receive your gift of pardon, and I thank you for a new life of intimacy with you through the Holy Spirit. Thank you for eternal life, in Jesus' name. Amen!

Congratulations! You've just made the best decision of your life! The lines of communication between you and the Father are now open! Your day-to-day salvation from all that attempts to come against you has just become fully available to you.

Ephesians 1:13 speaks of the promise, "And you also were included in Christ when you heard the message of truth, the gospel of your salvation. When you believed, you were marked in him with a seal, the promised Holy Spirit."

The Holy Spirit becomes our connection and communication with the Divine where every answer to health and wholeness lies. Who is the Holy Spirit anyway, and what does He offer us?

Heart Connection

1. Read the lyrics to "Mighty to Save" – Jeremy Camp.[3] I've provided a link for you here: https://www.azlyrics.com/lyrics/jeremycamp/mightytosave.html.

   Are any phrases resonating with you? If so, ask the Holy Spirit what He wants to communicate to you. In a journal, jot down what you hear.

2. Listen to the song "Mighty to Save."[4] I've provided a YouTube link for you here: https://youtu.be/YVeQoHdIDEE.

   What else is the Holy Spirit speaking to your heart? Be sure to write it down.

3. You may have already been a believer before picking up this book. Whether new to Christ or not, how does knowing you have open communication with God make you feel?

   Talk to God about your feelings and ask Him to speak something to your heart about how it makes Him feel to hear from you!

4. Was this the first time you've heard "The Good News"? If so, share the news of your salvation with other believers you know. They will rejoice with you! If you're not sure you know of anyone, you know me!

   I would love to hear from you! Contact me at www.mimikrogerauthor.com

5. Connecting to a church that shares the same beliefs you do is important in facilitating growth on your walk with Christ. Romans 1:11–12 says, "I long to see you so that I may impart to you some spiritual gift to make you strong—that is, that you and I may be mutually encouraged by each other's faith."

   If you've been a believer for some time, do you feel encouraged through relationships with other Christians? Are you part of a community of faith? If not, allow the Holy Spirit to direct you to the right place for you to fellowship with other believers.

   If you're a new believer, get connected! Ask the Holy Spirit to lead you to a church in your area that knows Him. Then, go! You'll be encouraged as you do.

Chapter 8

A Journey to Wholeness

If you're wondering how a loving God could allow His own Son to be brutally murdered, the answer lies in the Trinity. It was God Himself who hung on the cross through His Son, empowered by the Holy Spirit.

Is your head spinning yet?

The concept of the Trinity can be difficult to grasp, especially as we attempt to make sense of it with our earth-centered minds. The principle can only be apprehended with a spiritual lens that God gives. It's the Holy Spirit who helps us understand spiritual realities.

There is only One true God, and He expresses Himself in three persons. God comes to us as the Father, the Son, and the Holy Spirit. John 1:1 puts it simply, "In the beginning was the Word, and the Word was with God, and the *Word was God.*" A few passages later, in verse 14, it says, "The Word *became flesh* and made his dwelling among us." Jesus is the One who became flesh. He came to earth as a man.

Jesus told His disciples in John 14:9b–11, "Anyone who has seen me has seen the Father. How can you say, 'Show us the Father'? Don't you believe that I am in the Father, and that the Father is in me? The words I say to you I do not speak on my own authority. Rather, it is the Father, living in me, who is doing his work. Believe me when I say that I am in the Father and the Father is in me; or at least believe on the evidence of the works themselves."

The miracles Jesus performed are a testimony to His unity with the Father and so is the sinless life He led. For Him to combat the enemy and perform miracles, He was filled with the Holy Spirit. John 1:32 tells of the event, "Then John gave this testimony: 'I saw the Spirit come down from heaven as a dove and remain on him.' "

The same is true for us. We need the power of the Holy Spirit, working in us to overcome dysfunction and disease in our lives. After His ascension, Jesus was able to gift us with the Holy Spirit to live in and through us daily; so we can live connected to God and overcome the works of the enemy.

Jesus lived in unity with the Father in this way, and He makes that same phenomenon available to us. As we put our faith in Christ's atoning work, we also have the opportunity to have the indwelling Presence of the Holy Spirit so we can live health-filled and powerful lives.

The Holy Spirit helps us to know what God is like

The heart of God is that we know Him intimately. As we come to know His true nature, life returns to us—not only spiritually but also within our soul and body. To know God is to be loved and healed. To know Him is also to love Him in return; it becomes a natural consequence. All of His attributes and the ways in which He cares for us create instinctive gratitude.

A desire for a deeper connection, a real relationship, whereby communication flows between the Creator and those of His making, leads to an intimacy that goes beyond mere knowledge.

His love revealed through the Spirit, and to the heart of man, changes everything.

Paul the Apostle writes in Ephesians 3:16–19, "I pray that out of his glorious riches he may strengthen you with power *through his Spirit* in your inner being, so that Christ may dwell in your hearts through faith. And I pray that you, being rooted and established in love, may have power, together with all the Lord's holy people, *to grasp how wide and long and high and deep* is the love of Christ, and to know this *love that surpasses knowledge*—that you may be filled to the measure of all the fullness of God."

As I meditated on that Scripture, I sensed the Holy Spirit ask me to use my hands to grasp the love Paul spoke of. I spread my arms out wide. I then reached my hands forward to signify length, then I lifted them high and then dropped them low. At that moment, I realized I'd just motioned the cross.

Similarly, Psalm 103:11–12 speaks the same truth and also displays the cross, "*For as high as the heavens are above the earth*, so great is his love for those who fear him; *as far as the east is from the west,* so far has he removed our transgressions from us." The cross is laid out for us yet again.

Try it, you'll see!

The revelation of God's love and provision for us was settled at the cross. He goes beyond forgiveness and equips us to live in victory as we look to the Holy Spirit to guide and empower us forward. The gift of the Holy Spirit, and our unity with Him, bring health to our spirit, soul, and body.

I began to heal through Holy Spirit encounters

It was my own depravity that brought me to the feet of Jesus and into my own life-saving and born-again experience. I needed answers, a way out of the abusive cycle I was wrapped up in. Shame entered my life through sin and with it an unhealthy way of coping to gain the self-worth I'd foolishly given away as a late teen.

By the world's standards, I was a saint. After all, most of the other girls in my class had slept with several boys by now. Walking down the aisle on my wedding day in a white dress—symbolic of purity and virginity—would be an outright lie. When sex before marriage knocked on my door, in my short-sightedness, I answered without realizing the damage it would cause.

I married that same boy six months later, but my actions sealed a level of shame inside my soul that soon manifested in my physical body. A diagnosis of lupus came shortly after.

I hated myself for doing what I knew was wrong. My careless actions stared me in the face, and I felt its unending sting. In my mind's eye, I committed the ultimate sin. The enemy was more than thrilled to pounce on my weakness, to imbed his lies on the inside of me.

I heard the accuser's voice, much like a high-pitched screech capable of breaking glass, "You're dirty, defiled, a wicked wretch! There's no coming back from this." I felt his unceasing glare pierce my soul.

It wasn't the first time I'd heard the voice of the enemy. His shame and condemnation entered in years before my own poor choice. Shame began to cultivate its roots in childhood through high expectations and unrelenting discipline, and it didn't stop there.

The very thing my parents feared and tried to protect me from happened. An older boy molested me. There wasn't a moment of freedom from the devil's ridicule until the Holy Spirit came to my rescue.

Unlike the enemy had professed, a comeback was, in fact, available for every sin committed against me and for the failures I'd willingly walked into. It was in the power of Christ. Revelation 12:10 describes the hope we have in God, "Then I heard a loud voice in heaven say: 'Now have come the salvation and the power and the kingdom of our God, and the authority of his Messiah. For the accuser of our brothers and sisters, who accuses them before our God day and night, has been hurled down.' "

How did the Holy Spirit begin to bring about healing in my broken life and body? Let me share with you the journey.

Sin and shame was detrimental to my soul and body

Much like Adam and Eve, I was well aware of my nakedness. After my sexual sin and its resulting shame, I was consumed with a negative body image. Previously, how my body looked never crossed my mind.

I was caught up in a cycle of overeating, feeling incredibly guilty, and then either over-exercising or purging in unsuccessful attempts to remedy what I'd just done. It became all-consuming. An obsession with how my body looked began and held its grip on me far longer than even the eating disorder did.

My body betrayed me. It seemed to give in to temptation all too often. I despised how it looked, how it could never be perfect enough or thin enough. My body became my enemy. With all of its shortcomings, beginning with the sin it took part in, I despised every inch of it. In my unrenewed mind, my body fell short. How could it not? I bombarded it with unrealistic expectations of perfection.

A tree of self-hatred was birthed, with a trunk thick and wide. Its origin stemmed from the shame I carried, a result of the taboo sexual experience I'd chosen to participate in. The root grew over time, with overlapping strangling threads, producing life-sucking branches that consumed my life. The branches were the various coping measures I used in an attempt to relieve myself of the shame and pain.

I wasn't yet aware that a Savior had come to take my shame upon Himself.

I believe my body reacted to the self-hatred I carried by attacking itself.

An overactive immune system came into existence and took over. My body spoke back to the self-hatred it sensed in the only language it knew. In being attacked through vile thoughts, and my resulting actions toward it, my body reacted in like—with an immune system that invaded itself.

Often, events in the natural world represent a spiritual reality. I'm not proposing all autoimmune diseases are a result of sin, shame, or self-hatred. Lupus arises from a myriad of reasons, including not eating properly or lack of physical activity. I've also heard of individuals exposed to toxins and chemicals, which spurred on a continual immune response.

All I can speak from, with certainty, is what I've experienced personally—and share about the contributing factors to the illness which took over my own body. What I believed about myself—that I was shameful and deserved punishment—and how the enemy spoke to me with unkind words, which I believed were my own, was a big part of the dysfunction and disease I lived in.

As a result, I've learned the importance of combatting lies with truth. The One who brings that truth to us is the Holy Spirit!

Lies vie for attention but God's voice heals us

Even plants have been shown to respond to both positive and negative talk. IKEA conducted an experiment where two plants, under identical living conditions, received equal amounts of water, sunlight, and fertilizer.[1] Each plant also had looped voice recordings in their midst. The difference was in the words those recordings contained.

One plant received compliments and uplifting messages, while the other was bullied with hate-filled words. After thirty days, the plant inundated with negative talk showed signs of wilting.

Meanwhile, the plant that was spoken to kindly flourished and was healthy and strong.

The internal dialogue I carried was speaking death, and my body was listening—loud and clear. Lupus conceived and birthed in me what the enemy of my soul was spewing through degrading and ruthless thoughts.

It was a process to undo all the self-hatred I took in from the enemy's lies. Healing began as I turned my attention to the only One who could speak true life and worth to my wounded soul. He cleansed me from the guilt and condemnation I carried, from its inception at eighteen years old, when I chose to give away my virginity.

That shame morphed into body hatred and an eating disorder, which only exacerbated the judgments I already had against myself.

God's rescue from dysfunction

Tears welled up in my eyes and raced down each cheek as I stared at the vomit-covered throne that kept calling me back. I hated my behavior and despised myself for succumbing to the treachery yet again.

I hadn't yet discovered the existence of an Almighty throne that could lead me away from the insidious cycle. I didn't yet know the valiant Savior who took a powerful set of stripes on His back for my healing.

I remained in the frenzy of repetitive failure until God's unrelenting kindness and mercy came to my rescue. Without God's salvation, I was left in the trenches of a battle that gripped me to my core. The chaos enveloped my days until God cleansed me of my sin and made me new.

Your sin may be different than mine, but the way out is the same. God is truly the only One able to deliver us from dysfunction and the torment it produces. He does it by giving us wisdom, revelatory knowledge, and understanding into all Jesus provides for us.

Jesus is our lifeline.

I turned to God for help, and He answered me

In desperation, I cried out to God.

"God, are you real? If you are, will you please help me? I can't live like this anymore!"

His reply came after a grueling one-hour run, prompted by the enemy who first told me I had to pay for the ice cream I'd just eaten.

I slumped down on my '80s-style couch, covered with huge flowers in pastel hues.

If only I could feel as beautiful as those petals.

I took a moment to rest on them, untying the frayed laces of my sneakers, as I caught my breath.

Little did I know, the Breath of Life Himself was getting ready to answer the questions I'd asked of Him. Job 33:4 (ESV) reads, "The Spirit of God has made me, and the breath of the Almighty gives me life." His long-awaited entrance into my heart was coming to pass, and a life renewed by the power of the Holy Spirit in me with it.

I turned on the television and landed on a channel I'd never visited before. Humored by a woman who shot from the hip, I was drawn in. She seemed genuine and had a "tell it like it is" style, which I rather liked.

She was sharing about her life experiences and was relatable. When she spoke, my heart began to soften and open up. My ears perked up all the more when she began talking about God.

Was God answering my questions?

Was He real?

Was He willing to help me out of the degradation I was swallowed up in?

Reading God's Word opened up a new world to me

The television program I stumbled across that fateful day was called *Life in the Word*—as in the Word of God. Joyce Meyer confidently spoke, "You can have joy in your life, regardless of your circumstances." Intrigued by her style and the promise she mentioned, I followed her recommendation to read the Word of God daily.

A new excitement emerged as I began to investigate what the pages of Scripture had to share with me. They contained promises of life and freedom! I was learning what God's character was really like and beginning to grasp my value to Him. Out of that newfound insight, I treated not only myself differently but the people around me as well.

The keys to healing my broken heart were being revealed. A progression of doors to freedom began to open as I read God's Word. I once took refuge in food, the approval of others, and my own temporary achievements, but I now met a man who succeeded on my behalf, once and for all. His name was Jesus, and I was beginning to find out how real He was.

In my quiet bedroom, for hours at a time, I began to seek God through His written Word. I read the entire New Testament several times, along with many of the Psalms and Proverbs. Through the pages of Scripture, the Words I was reading spoke directly to my heart and soul. I felt as though they'd been written just for me.

I prayed continually for the fruit of the Spirit to be evident in my life, according to Galatians 5:22–23a (NLT), "But the Holy Spirit produces this kind of fruit in our lives: love, joy, peace, patience, kindness, goodness, faithfulness, gentleness, and self-control."

I knew I desperately needed each and every one of those delicious and satisfying fruits in my life to overcome what I'd been battling. What happened next spoke to me about how personal God really was.

He heard my prayers and was answering them!

When I felt the embrace of God, it changed everything

After watching Joyce Meyer's television program for a few weeks, I found out she was having a conference at a church in Colorado. I was thrilled that this woman—who had been instrumental in teaching me about God and the hope and life His Word contained for me—was coming to my very own hometown!

I sat a few rows back from the stage, enjoying the music. It was definitely not the type of church I was used to. I grew up Catholic, and to be honest, I only went to church when my dad forced me to go.

I felt as though I was at a concert rather than a church service. I surveyed the room and wondered why the songs' lyrics were being displayed on huge screens in front.

Where's the hymnal book, and why am I crying to the songs?

Soon, Joyce Meyer was on stage.

She pointed in my direction, "I'd like to pray for you, the one with the long curly hair."

Was that my spiral perm she was referring to?

Did she mean me?

Making her way back to my row, she walked straight up to me. She was much more petite than I gathered from her TV program. As she approached, I noticed her kind eyes. They dazzled with a beautiful hazel-green hue, but most noticeable was the love they gave off as she looked into mine. I felt her tenderness like a mother with a small child.

What she said next floored me—literally.

My legs instantly weakened when she placed her hand on my shoulder. I fell to the ground as I heard her pray the exact things I'd been asking God for.

She spoke with love and authority, combined into one. "Father, I pray your fruit of the Spirit to develop in your daughter as she seeks your face. Let her walk in your love, joy, peace, patience, kindness, goodness, faithfulness, gentleness, and self-control."

Wow, did she have that memorized?

More intriguing, *how did she know I'd been asking God for the fruit of the Spirit?*

I felt a peace come over me and a stillness I'd never experienced before. I began to weep, overcome by a love that was completely new to me.

God heard my prayers!

I felt the embrace of my God, who knew my heart's desires. He cared about them, about me—He wasn't mad at me.

When all I could see was my repetitive sin and shortcomings, He saw my heart. Psalm 51:17 (NLT) rang true, "The sacrifice you desire is a broken spirit. You will not reject a broken and repentant heart, O God."

God's unconditional love wiped away my pain

God's touch changed me. I couldn't exactly put to words what happened in my heart, but Matthew 11:28–30 already had, "Come to me, all you who are weary and burdened, and I will give you rest. Take my yoke upon you and learn from me, for I am gentle and humble in heart, and you will find rest for your souls. For my yoke is easy and my burden is light."

I was different. My soul had stumbled upon peace in the comfort of His touch. It spoke to me that God knew everything about me and loved me still. I skipped about with a joy that overflowed into every area of my life.

I later came across a postcard with a picture of a cat pawing at a fish inside a bowl. Below the scene was a Scripture: "The LORD your God is with you, the Mighty Warrior who saves. He will take great delight in you; in his love he will no longer rebuke you, but will rejoice over you with singing" (Zephaniah 3:17).

As I held the card in my hands and pondered it, I felt a nudge from above. It had described my unexpected experience with His Presence, as I read the lyrics on the big screens in church that day. It's the reason I was drawn to emotion and wept in my seat; His Presence does that. Without knowing it, God was singing over me. He then quieted my heart with His love as I melted into His personal touch.

My first encounter with His unconditional love set me on a path to reach for and experience more. I felt Him; His loving Presence was tangible—He was real.

I was on cloud nine for weeks, floating through life, without a care in the world! In the depths of my soul, I was made aware that I was known, accepted, and loved. Every detail of my life's actions laid bare before the Father, and He loved me anyway.

My healing had begun.

Heart Connection

1. Read the lyrics to "Holy Spirit" – Francesca Battistelli.[2] I've provided a link for you here: https://www.azlyrics.com/lyrics/francescabattistelli/holyspirit.html.

   Are any phrases resonating with you? If so, ask the Holy Spirit what He wants to communicate to you. In a journal, jot down what you hear.

2. Listen to the song "Holy Spirit."[3] I've provided a YouTube link for you here: https://youtu.be/UvBBC7-PSH0.

   What else is the Holy Spirit speaking to your heart? Be sure to write it down.

3. How is your self-talk? Do you realize when your thoughts have turned into a downward spiral?

   Write down the opposite of those thoughts and meditate on them. Bring your list out when you're being bombarded with lies from the enemy.

4. Have you ever felt the tangible Presence of the Holy Spirit? If so, think about your experience, and thank God for it. When we remind ourselves of our experiences with God, we can come into a place of sensing His Presence again.

   If you've never felt the Presence of the Holy Spirit, ask Him to show Himself to you in a tangible way. It's His pleasure to encounter you!

5. What sin, or pain in your life, needs cleansing by the power of the Holy Spirit? Psalm 23:3 (ESV) says, "He restores my soul. He leads me in paths of righteousness for his name's sake."

   God is willing to take what you give Him and bring restoration to your soul. He will trade your sin, shame, and pain for His righteousness. Bring what comes to mind to the Lord and invite Him to restore your soul.

Chapter 9

The Holy Spirit for You & Me

I began attending the church where I encountered that unforgettable touch from God. Soon, I was baptized in water, making a public proclamation of my faith. For the first time ever, someone explained to me the symbolism behind full immersion baptism.

A dark-haired woman excitedly taught, "When you go down into the water, you're being buried with Christ. You're dead to sin! When you rise up from the water, you've received cleansing and newness of life!"

She described what Romans 6:4 tells us, "We were therefore buried with him through baptism into death in order that, just as Christ was raised from the dead through the glory of the Father, we too may live a new life."

Even without having a full revelation of everything I was being taught, I was equally excited as the lady who told me all about it.

I later learned its significance at a deeper level. For now, I knew baptism was for me—and for good reason.

Jesus was baptized as an example for us to do the same

I was baptized as a baby, according to Catholic tradition, but I obviously didn't have a say in the matter. It was different now; I'd learned the meaning behind it all and was making the decision to be baptized for myself.

I felt all the more affirmed in my decision, knowing Jesus did it too.

Jesus was baptized solely as an example for us. He didn't need to be cleansed from sin because there wasn't any sin in Him. 1 John 1:5b says, "God is light; in him there is no darkness at all."

John the Baptist recognized Jesus' purity and was perplexed by His motivation to be baptized. He even attempted to dissuade Him, "But John tried to deter him, saying, 'I need to be baptized by you, and do you come to me?' Jesus replied, 'Let it be so now; it is proper for us to do this to fulfill all righteousness.' Then John consented" (Matthew 3:14–15).

The fact Jesus was baptized reminds me of the rubber wristbands I saw people wearing at church marked with the letters WWJD. They didn't exactly accent a dressy outfit properly, but people wore them nonetheless.

With their prevalence, on the wrists of so many, I finally broke down and inquired about them, even at the risk of sounding like a Christian novice—which I was.

Pointing to the blue rubber bracelet encircling his wrist, I asked the pastor, "What does that mean?"

"It stands for, what would Jesus do?"

"About what?" I asked.

Smirking, he said, "Jesus is to be our example in all things."

When Jesus was baptized, the Holy Spirit came and rested upon Him. "As soon as Jesus was baptized, he went up out of the water. At that moment heaven was opened, and he saw the Spirit of God descending like a dove and alighting on him" (Matthew 3:16).

I wanted the same for me too!

The Holy Spirit was given after Christ's ascension

The cross and resurrection represent for us the forgiveness of sins, a restored relationship with our Holy Father, and the gift of being sealed eternally with the Holy Spirit. The cross crucifies sin, so we can resurrect in newness of life with the Holy Spirit living within. It was after Christ's ascension when this gift of life was given.

Jesus said, "Nevertheless, I tell you the truth: it is to your advantage that I go away, for if I do not go away, the Helper will not come to you. But if I go, I will send him to you" (John 16:7 ESV).

Jesus was leaving the disciples to go back to His Father in Heaven, but He wasn't deserting them. He wouldn't leave them empty-hearted. His departure was necessary so that the Holy Spirit could take up permanent residence within them.

That reality remains true for every believer today.

The Holy Spirit becomes our constant Companion

Jesus chose to come to earth as a man and, as a result, could only be present with the disciples in His physical body. The coming of the Holy Spirit allowed for a completely different dynamic. He is Spirit, which enables Him to reside within the believer 24/7.

Jesus describes the role of the Holy Spirit in John 14:26 (ESV), "But the Helper, the Holy Spirit, whom the Father will send in my name, he will teach you all things and bring to your remembrance all that I have said to you."

The Holy Spirit reveals what God has done for us, "What we have received is not the spirit of the world, but the Spirit who is from God, so that we may understand what God has freely given us" (1 Corinthians 2:12).

The Holy Spirit brings understanding about Christ's righteousness for us, allowing restoration and connection with God. He further propels us to live according to our new identity in Him, providing the never-ending guidance and support of God Himself, expressed in the third person of the Trinity.

A constant indwelling Advocate, Teacher, and Counselor is available to us. He is an ever-present Companion and has the answer to any problem we face. We have full-time access to all-knowing counsel, the aid of Almighty God Himself!

As a friend of God, through Christ's righteousness, the company of the Holy Spirit never leaves. We are privy to Divine friendship and instruction from the indwelling Presence of the Holy Spirit, resting in our hearts.

Comfort and direction come from the Holy Spirit

Friends talk. They know what's going on in each other's lives. They advise, encourage, and just plain hang out. Our friends can bring to light what we might not see on our own; they may offer a different perspective.

The Holy Spirit enjoys sharing with us about God's perspective and His will for our lives. John 16:13 tells us, "But when he, the Spirit of truth, comes, he will guide you into all the truth. He will not speak on his own; he will speak only what he hears, and he will tell you what is yet to come."

A direct line of continual communication with the Heavens is part of our inheritance in Christ. We can ask God questions, and He will give us the truth, which leads us in the ways we are to go. Isaiah 30:21 says, "Whether you turn to the right or to the left, your ears will hear a voice behind you, saying, 'This is the way; walk in it.' "

The Holy Spirit gives inspiration, instruction, and strategy to overcome all manner of depravity, whether it's emotional or physical.

He acts as our healing balm, soothing all wounds. We can take our cares to Him, and He'll respond and comfort us. Anything that concerns us becomes His delight to take upon Himself. 1 Peter 5:7 instructs us, "Cast all your anxiety on him because he cares for you."

Our indispensable connection to the Holy Spirit defeats anything that attempts to come against all Jesus died and resurrected to give us. Eternal life is guaranteed, and so is abundant life here on earth.

John 10:10 describes the work of the enemy in contrast to God's work in our lives, "The thief comes only to steal and kill and destroy; I have come that they may have life, and have it to the full."

Living in the fullness of all Jesus died to give us is the God-given privilege of every person who puts their faith in Christ. An abundant life is for the believer who follows the leading of the Holy Spirit.

The Holy Spirit speaks to us about how we can have fruitful lives as we communicate with Him, and it's His pleasure to bless us.

1 Corinthians 2:9–10 (NLT) describes God's intention toward us, " 'No eye has seen, no ear has heard, and no mind has imagined what God has prepared for those who love him.' But it was to us that God revealed these things by his Spirit. For his Spirit searches out everything and shows us God's deep secrets."

The Holy Spirit brings life and transformation

We are a spirit; we have a soul, and we live in a body. Our spirit is the deepest part of who we are, and it's how we communicate with God because He is Spirit. We learn that God is Spirit early in Scripture. Genesis 1:2 enlightens us, "Now the earth was formless and empty, darkness was over the surface of the deep, and the *Spirit of God* was hovering over the waters."

It was God's Spirit, in conjunction with the spoken Word, that brought life to the earth, "And God said, 'Let there be light,' and there was light. God saw that the light was good, and he separated the light from the darkness" (Genesis 1:3–4).

The Spirit of God brings life and light to all that is dark. He continues to work, in the same way, today. When the Holy Spirit is invited to hover over our lives, newness of life springs forth and causes all desolation to depart.

When we become connected to the Father, through the Spirit indwelling our innermost being, we gain an internal compass that guides our lives out of depravity and into wholeness. As we are saturated and communicate with His Spirit, the transformation of what was once darkness comes into His light for healing.

This transformation is an impossibility until our spirit becomes alive to God. Through faith in Jesus' sacrificial obedience and all He accomplished through the cross and resurrection, we can receive life and intimacy with God. The Bible refers to this phenomenon as being *born-again.*

The born-again experience and what it means for us

John 3:1–7 explains, "Now there was a Pharisee, a man named Nicodemus who was a member of the Jewish ruling council. He came to Jesus at night and said, 'Rabbi, we know that you are a teacher who has come from God. For no one could perform the signs you are doing if God were not with him.' Jesus replied, 'Very truly I tell you, no one can see the kingdom of God unless they are born again.' 'How can someone be born when they are old?' Nicodemus asked. 'Surely they cannot enter a second time into their mother's womb to be born!' Jesus answered, 'Very truly I tell you, no one can enter the kingdom of God unless they are born of water and the Spirit. Flesh gives birth to flesh, but the Spirit gives birth to spirit. You should not be surprised at my saying, 'You must be born again.' "

In Jesus' conversation with Nicodemus, He explains the flesh is only capable of giving birth to flesh. It can only operate under the confines of its sinful nature and its destructive consequences passed down to us through Adam and Eve.

The Spirit of God gives birth to the spirit within us, giving us a new righteous nature in Christ, which allows us to live free from sin and death. It makes a connection to God and His Kingdom possible. His Heavenly Kingdom delivers an array of benefits, including the Holy Spirit, which brings us abundant life for today and unto eternity.

The born-again experience is the starting point to a relationship with a loving Father, and it makes a way out of the baseness of sin and its consequences. Romans 6:23 says, "For the wages of sin is death, but the gift of God is eternal life in Christ Jesus our Lord."

Sin has an eternal consequence—separation from God—but Christ saves us from it. Sin also affects the here and now. The Holy Spirit is our way out of its grip. Christ ignites within us the ability to hear from God and becomes our source for love, guiding us out of sin and death's grip.

Holy Spirit empowerment over darkness

1 Corinthians 10:13 encourages us, "No temptation has overtaken you except what is common to mankind. And God is faithful; he will not let you be tempted beyond what you can bear. But when

you are tempted, he will also provide *a way out* so that you can endure it."

The "way out" is through the voice of the Holy Spirit in our lives. Yielding to God's Spirit-to-spirit direction enables us to thwart all manner of destruction, attempting to keep us from receiving the promises of God over our lives. It brings us into a brand-new spiritual existence where Jesus, through the Holy Spirit, becomes the way for us to converse with God, who holds all of our answers.

Emotional and physical healing come into the light of God where revelation drives out the darkness. He leads us in exposing lies, giving us the truth instead. He teaches us about our identity and righteousness in Christ, which enables us to walk free from sin and in His purposes for our everyday lives—fueled by His grace.

Isaiah 11:2 speaks of what the Holy Spirit will do in the coming Messiah, Jesus. "The Spirit of the LORD will rest on him—the Spirit of wisdom and understanding, the Spirit of counsel and of might, the Spirit of the knowledge and fear of the LORD." The Holy Spirit does the same in and through us. He leads us into life and godliness.

2 Peter 1:3 puts it this way, "His divine power has given us everything we need for a godly life *through our knowledge of him* who called us by his own glory and goodness." He brings understanding regarding our righteous identity in Christ, which allows us to walk in His wisdom, making choices that reflect His holiness.

Choosing God's ways brings peace to our spirit, soul, and body. The good news is that we don't rely on our own strength to choose rightly. We rest in His power, working through us by the Spirit. Zechariah 4:6 entreats us to believe, " 'Not by might nor by power, but by my Spirit,' says the LORD Almighty."

The Holy Spirit burns all that hinders our lives through revelation, which comes by intimacy with Him. John the Baptist said about

Jesus in Luke 3:16c, "He will baptize you with the Holy Spirit *and* fire." The two go hand in hand.

The Presence of God encompasses His complete purity and holiness. It's all-consuming—like a fire. In Scripture, fire is used figuratively. Think about how God came to Moses in a burning bush (Exodus 3:2). Fire represents the transforming power that burns up all that's contrary to love's perfection.

What was lost through sin is brought back to us as we live through our new identity in Christ. Once that revelation defines us, it fuels us to follow the leading of the Holy Spirit. Our ability to reign in life comes first by way of knowing our righteousness in Christ, then by reliance on God's grace and the Holy Spirit's power to work in and through us.

I needed truth and fire in my life to overcome all that ailed me, and I was grateful God provided it for me through the Holy Spirit. My water baptism was an outward acceptance of His internal provision. It was also a signal to the kingdom of darkness that I now belonged to God's Kingdom.

Becoming part of a new Kingdom in Christ

Through water baptism, I chose to tell the world that I was a believer! My old state of being was transplanted with a life of devotion to the new King of my heart, and the supernatural world was being informed too.

Ephesians 2:1–2 explains, "As for you, you were dead in your transgressions and sins, in which you used to live when you followed the ways of this world and the ruler of the kingdom of the air, the spirit who is now at work is those who are disobedient."

I was getting ready to proclaim publicly that I was choosing to live for the Kingdom of Light rather than the kingdom of darkness. God had chosen me to be His by offering me His Son, and through water baptism, I was responding, "Yes, Papa, I'm yours!"

The Kingdom of Love and Light was just as exuberant at my choice to pledge allegiance to it and to God's work in my life. Luke 15:10 says, "In the same way, I tell you, there is rejoicing in the presence of the angels of God over one sinner who repents."

Jesus was showered with the love and acceptance of the Father at His baptism, as the Spirit came and rested on Him, "And a voice from Heaven said, *'This is my Son, whom I love; with him I am well pleased'* " (Matthew 3:17). The same precious gift was bestowed on me.

My own baptism was an opportunity to experience the Spirit of God coming to live in me and to know the love and delight of my Father as well. My cross-bought identity was ready for the taking. I was being made fully righteous through faith in His Son, and I wanted the world to know about it!

Welcome Holy Spirit, make me new!

I sat in a room filled with other fellow believers who had made the same decision I did. We were all getting water baptized.

As I waited my turn, a song I heard previously in church bubbled up in my heart. It was "Welcome Holy Spirit" by Mark Condon.[1] I recited the lyrics, over and over. Silently within, I sang, "Welcome Holy Spirit, we are in your Presence, fill me with your power, live inside of me..."

I marinated in those words, soaking in the tenderness of God's affection as I waited. I must have repeated them a hundred times, until the moment I was delicately interrupted by the church volunteer.

"Mimi, you're up next."

Isaiah 43:1 was in full swing and ready to be sealed, "I have summoned you by name; you are mine."

As my body was submerged in water, it was as if time stood still. I felt an overwhelming peace, much like the time Joyce Meyer prayed for me. Once again, I was drawn into the Presence of my Maker.

I believed what I'd been taught about baptism. Jesus was without sin, as 1 Peter 2:22 told me, "He committed no sin, and no deceit was found in his mouth." Through this symbolic act of water baptism, I was claiming the allocation of His perfection to me.

As I came up out of the water, I felt in the depths of my soul that a cleansing had taken place. I was made new! 2 Corinthians 5:17 confirmed what I experienced, "Therefore, if anyone is in Christ, the new creation has come: The old has gone, the new is here!"

The Spirit brought to life and made new what was once dark and dead—as He had done with the earth—in the beginning.

This time, He did it with me.

Heart Connection

1. Read the lyrics to "Welcome Holy Spirit" – Mark Condon.[2] I've provided a link for you here: https://lyricstranslate.com/en/mark-condon-welcome-holy-spirit-lyrics.html.

   Are any phrases resonating with you? If so, ask the Holy Spirit what He wants to communicate to you. In a journal, jot down what you hear.

2. Listen to the song "Welcome Holy Spirit."[3] I've provided a YouTube link for you here: https://youtu.be/ch-b1VkttqQ.

   What else is the Holy Spirit speaking to your heart? Be sure to write it down.

3. Are there times when you question if God hears you or if He speaks to you?

   If so, ask God what is hindering your communication with Him and how it can be changed. Then do what He is asking of you.

4. Like all relationships, if we don't spend quality time with people, we feel distant from them. Our relationship with God is no different.

   How can you cultivate consistent time with your Heavenly Father? Be specific and write your intentions down. Then, follow through!

5. It's empowering to know the Comforter and Counselor lives in you as a believer in Christ Jesus. How does that make you feel?

   Take some time to ask the Holy Spirit to comfort you regarding situations in your life, whether past or present. Ask Him for any guidance He has for you regarding those situations and what your next steps are.

Chapter 10

A Spiritual Language for Love & Power

Drenched from head to toe, I was enveloped in a sense of restored purity. I opened my mouth to give thanks, and strange words began to pour forth from my lips. I was speaking in a different tongue! A new language was birthed, along with my spirit, as I came up from the baptismal water.

God was speaking to me through the words that were coming from my lips. Every word made sense as I spoke them. They were messages directly from the heart of God to mine.

"You will go all over the world and help My children. You will lay hands on the sick and see them recover. You will have a son." Much more was said during this two-hour encounter with the Lord.

My future was being revealed to me by the One who would see to its attainment. The utterances I spoke came quickly, one word followed after another, like a rushing spring of water that couldn't be quenched. I felt refreshed from the inside out.

I was clean!

Filled with joy, I began to run, jump, and playfully dance. It all happened in the foyer of the church, right in front of everyone. For the first time since I could remember, I didn't care what anyone thought of me.

I heard the Lord say, "I'm letting you be the child you were never allowed to be." I was comforted by His Words, as they danced out of my own lips—right along with my feet—and into the atmosphere.

1 Corinthians 14:2 describes what I was experiencing, "For anyone who speaks in a tongue does not speak to people but to God. Indeed, no one understands them; they utter mysteries by the Spirit."

Several church members came up to me, wanting to explain what was going on.

"This is a prayer language, given by God; it's okay."

I giggled in response.

I knew it was God; I knew it was okay—I felt alive and free to be me!

To be seen, known, and spoken to by the One who made me gave me more pleasure than any other I'd yet found on earth. Psalm 84:10 says, "Better is one day in your courts than a thousand elsewhere." It was true!

I was in complete awe; the Creator of the Universe was conversing with me! It was what I'd been searching for my entire life, without knowing it.

I looked in a mirror while still speaking in the Heavenly language. I began to laugh with a depth of joy that was as foreign to me as the words I spoke. My cheeks were bright red, perhaps from the dancing, but I couldn't help thinking it was from the fire of God's transforming love reflecting off my skin.

My face was hot to the touch, and my entire body was wrapped in what felt like the warmth of a giant, all-encompassing blanket. It was as though He was hugging my body and soul in a sea of massive approval and care. To hear from God, to listen as He spoke His good plan for my life, to feel His heart of love and care for me; I couldn't help but be forever changed.

I skipped back into the sanctuary, knowing in my core that I was fully accepted. I felt a heavy burden of shame supernaturally lift off of me. There was a lightness with each step I took. The Breath of Life was present. It was as if the air in the atmosphere lifted each foot as though I were bouncing from one Heavenly cloud to another.

Drawn to the worship music roaring from the front of the church, I took a seat high up in the balcony. I was reminded that I was also spiritually sitting in Heavenly places. Ephesians 2:6 says, "And God raised us up with Christ and seated us with him in the heavenly realms in Christ Jesus."

My eyes caught the lyrics displayed on the big screens surrounding the stage. Line by line, I sang along, but not as written—I was singing in the Heavenly language I'd been given.

I began to grow in all God had for me

I only knew about speaking in tongues from my New Testament reading over the few weeks prior. I'd never talked to anyone about it or witnessed another person actually speaking it. It wasn't anything I'd given much thought to.

In fact, it hadn't even made my prayer list—or had it?

I later thought, perhaps God considered the song I repeated as I waited for my turn to be baptized as a prayer? After all, I was singing, "Welcome Holy Spirit." Whether by deliberate request or not, it happened! I'm so glad it did because it helped me to know how real and personal God was once again.

I went on to realize, my first experience with tongues wasn't the norm. Even though I had easily conversed with God and understood all He was relaying to me that day, it didn't continue as such.

For a few weeks after the initial encounter, I found myself uttering only two or three words. I also didn't have the faintest idea as to their meaning! The robust vocabulary and conversation I initially had with God diminished.

1 Corinthians 14:4a says, "Anyone who speaks in a tongue edifies themselves." So I knew it was important to continue in it. It was an act of faith for me to speak out the few words I was left with. I had to learn, even in the moments when I didn't tangibly feel God's Presence or understand the language I was speaking in, He was still working inside of me and lifting me up.

As I continued to pursue all God had for me, in hearing from and relating with Him, I began to grow. It was the same with my prayer language; I was almost like a toddler who only knows a few words at first. Eventually, the few words I did have grew into many more.

As I prayed in tongues, thoughts entered my mind, which prompted me to pray them in English. So I did. I then went back to praying in tongues. They seemed to be feeding off of one another. I wondered if I might be receiving interpretation by way of the English prayers that emanated from the words I spoke in tongues.

Either way, I knew it was good for me. 1 Corinthians 14:15 encouraged me, "So what shall I do? I will pray with my spirit, but I will also pray with my understanding; I will sing with my spirit, but I will also sing with my understanding."

Tongues for God's will and for continual prayer

When we speak in tongues, it elicits direct communication with God. They are prayers that enter God's throne room and are answered because they're in direct alignment with His perfect will.

I believe, when we pray in the Spirit, it accelerates God's plan for our lives because we're praying in agreement with what He wants for us. 1 John 5:14–15 states, "This is the confidence we have in approaching God: that if we ask anything *according to his will, he hears us.* And if we know that he hears us—whatever we ask—we know that we have what we asked of him."

The Word of God tells us His good and perfect will for us. God's Word divides our own ideas, coming from our soul, from His perfect truth. Our soul encompasses our mind, will, and emotions. Generally, I don't know what I'm praying in tongues. My own will and intellect are inactive. It assures me, I'm praying in accordance with God's will.

Hebrews 4:12 explains, "For the word of God is alive and active. Sharper than any double-edged sword, it penetrates even to *dividing soul and spirit*, joints and marrow; it judges the thoughts and attitudes of the heart." There's a distinct division between our soul and the Spirit. Much like a bone and the marrow it contains, they are two separate entities.

As I prayed in tongues, I found my mind could be on other things at the same time. Making a grocery list or planning dinner happened as I prayed in the Spirit. It showed me my mind and Spirit were separate from one another. 1 Corinthians 14:14 confirmed my finding, "For if I pray in a tongue, my spirit prays, but my mind is unfruitful."

This reality is exceptionally useful! The separation of mind and Spirit makes 1 Thessalonians 5:17 possible, "Pray continually." The only way I can pray without ceasing, and accomplish the other things I need to do in life, is through praying in the Spirit since I can do it while engaging my mind on other things.

I was also certain to have my prayers answered because I was surely speaking God's Word back to Him without my soul's involvement. The practicality and effectiveness of praying in tongues were undeniable as was the encouragement and power I felt in practicing it.

Tongues for powerful warfare and worship

In my early days as a new believer, I worked at a package delivery company in the small sorting department. We were in charge of organizing small packages into their correct bins. One of my co-workers was pregnant and worked next to me. We took our posts next to the conveyer belt and turned boxes and packages right-side-up as they rushed by.

Suddenly, I saw her lay her hands on her belly. She winced in pain, and her knees buckled as she steadied herself on the steel bar encasing the conveyer belt. I instinctively put my hands over hers and began to pray in tongues. I prayed internally; she couldn't hear me.

I was in the awkward, two-to-three words stage of speaking in tongues. So I was surprised what I heard bubble up inside of me, a flow of words similar to my first experience at my baptism. I didn't have an interpretation, but I felt a sense of empowerment in the atmosphere. I knew I was praying for God's will.

Within moments, my co-worker was completely well and returned to flipping boxes right alongside me. I began to realize this speaking in tongues thing was powerful against the work of the enemy!

Years after my kidney transplant, I once had a two-week bout of anxiety reminiscent of some of my past experiences. My mind raced as it once had before. I felt helplessly bound to it. This time, medication wasn't to blame. I had no idea where it was coming from.

I didn't feel like being around anyone but hoped if I went to church and immersed myself in worship, it might help. Instead, the anxiety became worse! I sat next to a woman who sang annoyingly loudly and off-key. The distraction was too much to bear in my current state. It's almost as though the annoyance was mimicking what was going on within—a continual taunting.

I asked my husband to take me home and encouraged him to return to the service. The moment I walked into my house, I felt an urgency in my spirit to pray in tongues. As I did, I felt prompted to do something that seemed incredibly silly, but I was desperate. I'd do just about anything to get out of this state of unrelenting chaos.

I began to stab the air with an invisible sword, speaking aloud the utterances shooting from my mouth. I'm glad I suggested my husband return to church because I'm not certain I would've behaved in this way if he were home.

As I thrust the sword in the air, I imagined my enemy's slaughter. I fought so fiercely, in Word and action, that I became breathless and tired as if I'd just run a mile. Covered in sweat, I dropped to my knees, weary from the battle.

I suddenly felt a shift in the atmosphere. I knew I was praising God for the victory as I continued to pray in tongues. At that moment, I felt the heaviness leave me. Whatever it was that attacked my mind, stole my peace, and disintegrated my joy—was gone.

The oppression lifted.

The Bible says we praise God when speaking in tongues (1 Corinthians 14:16). Worship is powerful against the works of the enemy in our lives. As we put our attention on God, we're exalting Him above our circumstances. In these moments of honoring and worshipping God, we're communicating our trust in Him to see us through and defeat what is coming against us.

God equips us with His Spirit and goes before us in every spiritual battle we find ourselves in. Psalm 23:4–5a reminds us, "Even though I walk through the darkest valley, I will fear no evil, for you are with me; your rod and your staff, they comfort me. You prepare a table before me in the presence of my enemies."

I've often sensed a boldness and courage come over me when I've prayed in tongues; it's as though I've entered into a war against the demonic spiritual realm and won!

I've found myself using tongues as a weapon of defense, but praying in the Spirit is also described as an offensive weapon in Scripture. "Pray in the Spirit at all times and on every occasion. Stay alert and be persistent in your *prayers for all believers everywhere*" (Ephesians 6:18 NLT).

I was once told that when praying in the Spirit, I may actually be praying for someone I don't even know, possibly in a different country! What an interesting thought. That means I, too, may be receiving prayer from a person that doesn't know me. God could be implementing battle plans from the lips of another, on my behalf, and I might be doing the same for them.

I believe praying in tongues is for every believer

If praying in the Spirit does all the Bible speaks to us about, then I'm convinced it's for anyone who has the Holy Spirit living within.

It's simply a call to pray, which is for every believer. Mark 16:17 assures us, "And these signs *will accompany those who believe*: In my name they will drive out demons; *they will speak in new tongues.*"

Prayer keeps us and others safe from harm!

When our hearts are heavy or confusion surrounds us, praying in tongues comes to our aid. Romans 8:26–27 says, "The Spirit helps us in our weakness. We do not know what we ought to pray for, but the Spirit himself intercedes for us through wordless groans. And he who searches our hearts knows the mind of the Spirit, because the Spirit intercedes for God's people in accordance with the will of God."

Praying in tongues produces the perfect prayer!

If you have yet to experience praying in the Spirit, ask God for it. He is faithful to His Word and will give you what is rightfully yours as a believer in Christ.

The Bible talks about different types of tongues

There are other tongues the Bible refers to, different than our prayer language. It's referred to as a gift and is for use in public. It's a message given, to a believer, in a Heavenly language from God for His people. It requires an interpretation, which is also a gift through the Holy Spirit. It is given to bring understanding to those receiving the message.

1 Corinthians 14:6 says, "Now, brothers and sisters, if I come to you and speak in tongues, what good will I be to you, unless I bring you some revelation or knowledge or prophecy or word of instruction?"

The interpretation of a tongue, received in the Spirit, brings meaning to language the human mind cannot comprehend. 1 Corinthians 14:23 says, "So if the whole church comes together and everyone speaks in tongues, and inquirers or unbelievers come in, will they not say that you are out of your mind?"

It's important to recognize that there's a clear distinction between a tongue that produces a message from God that is for the edification of others and your own personal prayer language.

Generally, our Heavenly prayer language tongue is to be a private conversation with God. It's the reason I prayed under my breath, rather than out loud, during the incident with my co-worker.

God provides, in your personal prayer language tongue, the ability to pray silently. People around you won't have a clue that you're praying at all! This is incredibly helpful if you find yourself in a dark situation, needing Holy Spirit help. You're able to pray anywhere and anytime, without detection and without people thinking you're crazy!

1 Corinthians 14:28 instructs, "If there is no interpreter, the speaker should keep quiet in the church and speak to himself and to God." Only when a tongue rises up from the Holy Spirit for the edification or instruction of others should it be spoken aloud.

An interpretation is to follow so that intelligible encouragement will touch the lives of believers and unbelievers alike.

The Bible also speaks of tongues, coming upon people, in the form of an earthly foreign language. It becomes a sign to the one hearing their own language spoken to them by someone who isn't native to it.

Acts 2:6–8 describes such a scenario, "When they heard this sound, a crowd came together in bewilderment, because each one heard their *own language being spoken.* Utterly amazed, they asked: 'Aren't all these who are speaking Galileans? Then how is it that *each of us hears them in our native language?*' "

The purpose of such a sign and wonder is to bring people to believe in God. The Holy Spirit is making Himself known to be real and at work among them.

Baptism of the Holy Spirit comes in God's timing

Our experiences with the Father are unique to who we are and what we need to reign in life. Our encounters with Him are as individual as the fingerprints He gives us. The One who intricately made us, and continues to provide us with all things, has the will and power to provide everything we need—when and how we need it.

I happened to receive my prayer language at the time of my water baptism. This isn't always the case. The Bible speaks to this in the book of Acts when Paul is traveling to Ephesus. On his way, he ran into twelve *disciples*, "and asked them, 'Did you receive the Holy Spirit *when you believed?*' They answered, 'No, we have not even heard that there is a Holy Spirit' " (Acts 19:2).

The Scripture makes clear that the people Paul talked to were already believers. In fact, they are referred to as disciples. As their conversation continues, we discover there's more than one baptism. "So Paul asked, 'Then what baptism did you receive?' 'John's baptism,' they replied" (Acts 19:3).

Paul then explains and teaches them, "John's baptism was a baptism of repentance. He told the people to believe in the one coming after him, that is, in Jesus" (Acts 19:4). These disciples knew who Jesus was and followed after Him as many do in the church today. However, they were missing one key ingredient that helps to flourish intimacy with Christ and gives power to reign in life—the baptism of the Holy Spirit.

Let's look at their response, "On hearing this, they were baptized in the name of the Lord Jesus. When Paul placed his hands on them, the Holy Spirit came on them, and they spoke in tongues and prophesied" (Acts 19:5–6).

Jesus instructed His disciples to wait for the Holy Spirit, as it would come to them only after His ascension. "Do not leave Jerusalem, but wait for the gift my Father promised, which you have heard me speak about" (Acts 1:4b).

The fulfillment of the gift came through Jesus with fire just as John the Baptist prophesied in Luke 3:16. We hear about it in Acts 2:3–4, "They saw what seemed to be tongues of fire that separated and came to rest on each of them. All of them were filled with the Holy Spirit and began to speak in other tongues as the Spirit enabled them."

The baptism of the Spirit was for believers in Jesus' day, and it's still available today. It's a gift, left unopened by many.

Needless division over the baptism of the Spirit

The subject of the baptism of the Spirit, as a separate event from salvation, has brothers and sisters in Christ on two sides of the same fence.

On one side are those believing you automatically receive the Holy Spirit upon belief. Ephesians 1:13 clearly states, "And you also were included in Christ when you heard the message of truth, the gospel of your salvation. When you believed, you were marked in him with a seal, the promised Holy Spirit." There's no doubt that a person's spirit comes alive to God when they receive Christ—it's what it means to be born-again.

Standing on the other side of the fence are those insisting a separate encounter brings Holy Spirit power. Could it be, both sides are correct? There needn't be a fence of separation among those who believe.

The idea that God is so grand and cannot be boxed into any yard of human limitation is a freeing one. I'm willing to humble myself enough to simply ask for the fullness of what God has for me and leave it at that. If you'd like that too, I invite you to pray the following prayer with me:

Father God, I want all you have for me through the Holy Spirit. I thank you for coming to me when I first received the gift of your blood sacrifice on my behalf. Thank you that I was born-again and made alive to your Spirit. I surrender myself to you completely. I desire the fullness of what you've made available, including my own Heavenly prayer language and all the other gifts you have for me, through the power of the Holy Spirit. I thank you for the blessing your gifts provide and pray they glorify you in my life. I ask to be filled continually by your Spirit every day, in every way. In Jesus' name, I pray. Amen!

Heart Connection

1. Read the lyrics to "More Love, More Power" – Michael W. Smith.[1] I've provided a link for you here: https://www.azlyrics.com/lyrics/ michaelwsmith/morelovemorepower.html.

   Are any phrases resonating with you? If so, ask the Holy Spirit what He wants to communicate to you. In a journal, jot down what you hear.

2. Listen to the song "More Love, More Power."[2] I've provided a YouTube link for you here: https://youtu.be/MhnmLNfyqY4.

   What else is the Holy Spirit speaking to your heart? Be sure to write it down.

3. Have you heard about speaking in tongues before reading this book? If so, what are your beliefs surrounding it?

   If you feel hesitant, ask the Holy Spirit to reveal to you its importance. I encourage you to continue to pray and study what the Word of God has to say about it.

   If you already speak in tongues, reminisce with the Lord over some experiences you've had with Him in this area.

4. Have you ever been gifted the interpretation of a tongue, either for yourself or in a public setting? 1 Corinthians 14:13 (NLT) says, "So anyone who speaks in tongues should pray also for the ability to interpret what has been said."

   Do this now. Ask the Holy Spirit to give you the interpretation next time you pray in tongues, or if you hear a tongue being spoken from someone else.

5. This chapter has revealed the many benefits of utilizing the Heavenly prayer language God gives to believers. I believe the enemy may be part of the opposition the baptism of the Holy Spirit has had among different denominations because of the love and power it provides.

   If you already speak in tongues, list some benefits you've received through prayer.

   If you're awaiting your prayer language, be at rest in God's perfect timing for you and thank Him in advance for what He will do.

Chapter 11

Your Righteous Identity

The word disease is simply dis-*ease*. A lack of rest in our soul affects our health and body. Rest in soul comes through knowing our righteousness.

The devil will eat us for lunch if our righteousness in Christ isn't firmly established. It's Christianity 101—righteousness in Christ alone. Our right standing with God is not based on anything other than who Jesus is for us. It cannot be bought or received through striving. In fact, it's the exact opposite—it's a gift.

Living fixed on who Christ is for us keeps our souls at peace. Our new identity in Him propels us to live in the righteous nature we've been given. That revelation keeps us from giving in to temptation—which also causes dis-*ease* and disease.

A heart change came the moment I received Christ

I had plenty of reasons to lack deep soul rest before meeting the Lord. Over time, as a new believer, my soul came under a different type of attack.

Before accepting the Lord, I sinned without a second thought. I'd cut someone off in traffic and think it was absolutely warranted.

Serves them right; they shouldn't have been driving so fast!

I never thought twice when judging someone's actions while galloping on my own darkened high horse.

Once the Holy Spirit took up residence, I began to learn the Word of God. As I became more versed in the Bible, my awareness of sin increased. The result was something called conviction, but the devil pounced on it and turned it into condemnation.

As a new believer, God's good nature had been placed in my spirit and awoke new sentiments and desires. I actually noticed when I was behaving pridefully. That was new!

My awareness level regarding what was right and wrong was all of a sudden front and center. I was miserable because even with my heftiest efforts, I still failed. The list grew longer and longer as I became aware of love's expectations based on Scripture.

Jesus says in Matthew 7:13–14, "Enter through the narrow gate. For wide is the gate and broad is the road that leads to destruction, and many enter through it. But small is the gate and narrow the road that leads to life, and only a few find it."

The more I learned from the Bible about sin, the size of my gate became meticulously small. My size eight shoes scarcely fit on this newfound road of Christ's perfection. I was downtrodden with new pressures, in addition to the old soul wounds that caused false belief systems I had yet to deal with.

When I was oblivious to God's ways and the narrow path, I felt rather justified in my loveless dealings with people. Now, everything was different. As a follower of Christ, with a new nature, I was compelled to behave in a way that honored Him. Not because I had to, but because I wanted to!

After meeting the Lord, I was blessed to have received freedom from an eating disorder. I experienced his mercy and unconditional acceptance. It's what set me free! Additionally, my soul had been anchored by Him through a scary lupus diagnosis. He infused me with hope and strength throughout my journey. He even blessed me with the promise of eternal life with Him!

As a result, I wanted to love Him in return. 1 John 4:19 says, "We love because he first loved us." It's true! With all my heart, I found my deepest desire was to live differently. I wanted to be like Him, evidenced through my prayers to walk in the fullness of the fruit of the Spirit.

Every failed attempt left me dejected and rejected. My prayer became Psalm 51:12, "Restore to me the joy of your salvation and grant me a willing spirit, to sustain me." God wasn't disappointed in me or rejecting me; rather, I poured those destructive emotions upon myself—with the help of the devil, of course.

I willingly walked myself into the adversary's playground of ruthless expectations that God never called me to. I hated my behavior and rejected myself because of it. When lupus hit shortly thereafter, it was an outward sign of what was going on internally. It was the straw that broke the camel's back, but its ascent began long before that.

It started with a childhood full of pressure and the shame that came with harsh consequences for misbehavior. It grew from there by way of another person's sin against me through molestation.

My own poor choices followed as a teen, likely driven by the shame and lack of value I felt from my previous life's experiences. I used overexercising and bulimia in an attempt to get the perfect body, thinking I would gain self-worth. Mistreatment of my body along with all the shame and emotional turmoil trapped inside my soul were certainly contributing factors to lupus.

God saved me from continuing in the cycle of pain and shame from my past by making Himself known to me. I was brand-new, free, and felt alive! Soon after, the honeymoon was over and what started as a relationship through my first God-encounter somehow turned into the requirements of religion.

An exhausting attempt to live rightly, based on my own efforts, began to creep in; with it came an onslaught of demonic accusation and judgment.

Jesus came to rescue us, not to condemn us

The devil had John 14:15 glare at me, square in the eyes, every time I failed, "If you love me, keep my commands." He was always ready to pounce on my heart by twisting Scripture.

Sadly, I wasn't yet fully rooted in Christ's righteousness for me. For far too many years of my Christian walk, my prayer journal was filled with "God, please forgive me" and "Lord, I did it again! I'm so sorry." I wasn't fixed on who I was in Christ and who God was for me.

I turned to the lane of performance I once had in the world into one with God. I traveled on a highway of continual regret and disappointment, which took a toll on my soul and body. Somehow, I quickly forgot what I learned at the beginning, which brought me to God in the first place—His unconditional love.

I forgot the Holy Spirit was my Advocate; He was on my side to help, not to condemn me. Jesus was my Defender, not my judge. These Words came straight from my Savior's lips, "If anyone hears my words but does not keep them, I do not judge that person. For I did not come to judge the world, but to save the world" (John 12:47).

I needed to be reminded of the simplicity of the Gospel, also described perfectly in Romans 5:8, "But God demonstrates his own love for us in this: While we were still sinners, Christ died for us."

One of the most detrimental attacks on our health comes by way of shame and condemnation. Shame and condemnation wreak havoc because, if we allow it, they can keep us from the Presence of God. The Holy Spirit is our Helper, so staying connected to Him is vital.

We've already explored the account of Adam and Eve and how sin, and its resulting shame, had them running away from God instead of toward Him.

Every story in the Bible isn't simply a story. The Bible is a Heavenly instruction manual for daily living. If we regard passages in this way, every story carries within its plot and resolution the potential to be our greatest resource for healthy living.

There is only one accuser, and it's not God!

Satan loves for God's children to fester in the unauthorized shame he brings in the aftermath of poor decisions. His plans are to steal our joy because he knows it will also rob us of strength. Nehemiah 8:10c states, "Do not grieve, for the joy of the LORD is your strength."

We must continue in the joy of the Lord, based on who He is for us, so we can keep our strength and freely run to Him in time of need. The fact that God constantly delights in us permits us to go to Him for the wisdom and grace we need in order to overcome.

Satan is referred to as the "accuser" (Revelation 12:10). He continually waves a pointed finger, with the goal of blocking our fellowship with God. He does it to keep us from communicating with the only One who can help us. The enemy of our soul wants us to believe God is mad at us.

The devil is a liar. "He was a murderer from the beginning, not holding to the truth, for there is no truth in him. When he lies, he speaks his native language, for he is a liar and the father of lies" (John 8:44b–c). The devil will always do what is natural to him, which is to lie. God continues to do what is natural to Him, which is to love.

Nothing can keep us from the love of God. Romans 8:38–39 says, "For I am convinced that neither death nor life, neither angels nor demons, neither the present nor the future, nor any powers, neither height nor depth, nor anything else in all creation, will be able to separate us from the love of God that is in Christ Jesus our Lord."

It's in this place of God's unconditional love where we receive hope for a better future. Christ's righteousness for us is our defense from the enemy and his lies. Colossians 2:15 (TPT) describes Christ's victory, which becomes ours, "Then Jesus made a public spectacle of all the powers and principalities of darkness, stripping away from them every weapon and all their spiritual *authority and power to accuse us.* And by the power of the cross, Jesus led them around as prisoners in a procession of triumph. He was not their prisoner; they were his!"

In Christ, we remain acceptable to God regardless of our behavior and are deemed not guilty. The enemy's condemnation is illegal. Romans 8:1 says, "There is now no condemnation for those who are in Christ Jesus." Our spirit can get crushed under the weight of condemnation—only if we allow it.

No fear of punishment in God's perfect love

The very temptation the enemy uses to entices us, he then immediately turns around and attempts to condemn us with it. It's up to us to hold our ground against him. Ephesians 6:14 (NLT) tells us how, "Stand your ground, putting on the belt of truth and the body armor of God's righteousness."

Our unchangeable right standing with God must be proclaimed through faith, especially when the enemy comes with his accusations and enticements. The Word of God, taken in through the life-producing Holy Spirit, has the power to train us in the ways of Christ and His righteousness for us. It's how we defeat the enemy's lies. We can remain steadfast in the righteousness Christ bought for us with His blood and know our Father accepts His sacrifice on our behalf.

God's love has no strings attached; He really does love us without conditions. It's hard for us to grasp because our lives have often shown us that love is conditional. Conditional love brings with it the fear of punishment, but God gave His Son to take sin's penalty upon His own body for us, so we have nothing to fear.

1 John 4:18 says, "There is no fear in love. But perfect love drives out fear, because fear has to do with punishment. The one who fears is not made perfect in love." Unconditional love is perfect love. If we know we're loved in this way, fear has no place in our lives.

Our assurance stems from who Jesus is for us—our righteousness. "But now God has shown us a way to be made right with him without keeping the requirements of the law, as was promised in the writings of Moses and the prophets long ago. We are made right with God by placing our faith in Jesus Christ. And this is true for everyone who believes, no matter who we are" (Romans 3:21–22 NLT).

Repentance is still necessary as a Christian

Our righteousness in Christ was settled the moment we put our faith in Jesus as our Savior. As a new believer, I went overboard, making repentance my main focus, when God and what He'd already accomplished for me was to take preeminence. The Lord wanted me to fellowship with Him, not my sins.

That didn't mean I wasn't supposed to repent after sinning, but He wanted me to do so while staying in the place of love and righteousness Jesus had already paid for me to have.

A relationship, whether with God or another person, thrives on the same principles.

If I were to hurt my husband somehow, I would apologize to him and turn away from behaving that way again. His gift to me would be in forgiving me, and our love would remain steadfast through it all.

It's the same in our relationship with God. We're to acknowledge the wrong we've done and quickly accept God's gift of love and forgiveness. We don't need to beat ourselves up over our failures. Jesus already endured that pain for us at the hands of Roman soldiers.

Just as righteousness is a precious gift, so is repentance. It's based on the kindness of God and has nothing to do with punishment.

Romans 2:4 says, "Or do you show contempt for the riches of his kindness, forbearance and patience, not realizing that God's *kindness* is intended to lead you to repentance?" When we recognize sin, we're to ask for forgiveness from our loving Father. Then, let it go by faith, trusting in the work Jesus has already done for us through the cross.

1 John 1:9 says, "If we confess our sins, he is faithful and just and will forgive us our sins and purify us from all unrighteousness." I always confessed my sin but never stopped long enough to receive the purification God offered. He was willing to soothe my soul in the aftermath of sin by way of His loving Presence; He wanted to wash me clean and comfort me in the process.

Repentance is an act of humility, whereby we gain wisdom for future occasions when the devil comes to tempt us. We benefit from the unconditional love of God, who tenderly restores us and teaches us a better way as we listen for direction from the Holy Spirit.

Without a solidly rooted system of righteousness, the enemy had me wallowing in guilt, and I continually focused on my failures instead of the faithful provision of the Father through Jesus Christ. Righteousness in Christ ensures my relationship with God remains unhindered, no matter what.

God offers us peace as we allow ourselves to receive His grace and revelation of righteousness in and through His perfect Son. It produces rest in our soul, and our bodies naturally follow suit, but we must believe it.

I had to know, deep in my heart, after giving in to temptation that I was always welcome to come into the arms of my kind Father. As I turn my attention to Him, it becomes an opportunity for my emotions and will to fall in line with His. Remember, God is still Holy and desires holiness in our lives. He makes provision for that, too, in Christ.

Knowing you're a saint helps you act like one

Reminding ourselves of who we are in Christ further propels us to behave in line with who God has proclaimed us to be. He calls us saints because of our unity with Christ.

Before Jesus' crucifixion, He prays to God, "*I am in them* and you are in me. May they experience such perfect unity that the world will know that you sent me and that you love them as much as you love me" (John 17:23 NLT). Jesus' purity in us makes it possible to look upon the face of our Heavenly Father without shame. It allows access to His Presence, which transforms us and leads us toward paths of life and righteousness.

Believers are called saints in the New Testament over sixty times, sixty-seven to be exact.[1] Believing it applies to you and me makes all the difference in how we live. If you think you're a worm, you'll behave like one! A renewing of our old mindsets must take place.

What we believe about who Jesus is for us and who we are in the sight of God as a result, matters! The challenge is to allow our identity to be based on the truth of God's Word alone and never on our behavior or our own striving to produce righteousness.

Colossians 2:6 says, "So then, just as you received Christ Jesus as Lord, continue to live your lives in him." We came into a relationship with Christ through faith in God's goodness, and that's the same way in which we're to live.

Galatians 5:4 describes the fate of a believer without the revelation of living based on Christ's righteousness alone, "You who are trying to be justified by the law have been alienated from Christ; you have fallen away from grace." The gift of God's grace has many facets. It's receiving what we don't deserve, but it's also empowerment to do what we can't on our own.[2]

Living righteously is possible as we align our thinking

As our root system goes from trying to trusting, the freedom to live rightly flows. It's important because the result of living righteously is a healthy soul and body.

We must renew our minds to the reality of Christ in us if we are to do as James 1:22–24 exhorts, "Do not merely listen to the word, and so deceive yourselves. Do what it says. Anyone who listens to the word but does not do what it says is like someone who looks at his face in a mirror and, after looking at himself, goes away and immediately forgets what he looks like."

As we look in the mirror of Christ and His righteousness for us, our potential to live out holiness becomes ours. Galatians 2:20 anchors this reality, "I have been crucified with Christ and I no longer live, but Christ lives in me. The life I now live in the body, I live by faith in the Son of God, who loved me and gave himself for me."

Freedom from the chains of dysfunction is made available to anyone willing to receive it by faith. It is indeed an act of faith because every time we give in to temptation, we question the gift. We must believe in the truth of our new identity in Christ and through that we will behave righteously.

Our belief system affects how we behave. Knowing we've already been made completely righteous in Christ is the springboard to living it out. Romans 12:2 instructs us, "Do not conform to the pattern of this world, but be transformed by the *renewing of your mind*. Then you will be able to test and approve what God's will is—his good, pleasing and perfect will."

Living in a godly way is only possible as we renew our mind to the Gospel; Jesus accomplished our purity for us. As we grab hold of its truth in our minds, our hearts can run freely in knowing we're completely saturated with God's fullness and life. Our godly behavior naturally flows out of that belief.

It takes a renewing of the mind because experience has shown us, we're far from acting like saints. At some point, if we're to live a victorious life, we must let go of what feels true and choose to believe what the Word of God says.

We're made saints in His likeness by His grace. If we're to overcome sin and its death producing consequences, we must line up with the truth about who we are now in Christ.

Living like Jesus in this world

As we set our minds on the Word of God and its truth, the freedom to live righteously becomes a reality. 1 John 4:17 shares the good news, "This is how love is made complete among us so that we will have confidence on the day of judgment: In this world we are like Jesus."

As I take hold of that truth, I will mirror the nature of Jesus in my life. If I associate myself with the character of God that's been made fully attainable and alive in me, then I will react naturally out of that state of being. When the devil comes with a temptation to have me do something outside of love's parameters, whether toward myself or another person, I can tell Him that's not who I am.

I must be fully convinced Who it is I belong to and Who I'm like as a result of my connection and relationship to Jesus. This supernatural reality is stated clearly for us in Colossians 2:9–10, "For in Christ all the fullness of the Deity lives in bodily form, and in Christ you have been brought to fullness. He is the head over every power and authority."

As He is, so are we in this world because He fills us with Himself.

1 Corinthians 3:16 tells us, "Don't you know that you yourselves are God's temple and that God's Spirit dwells in your midst?"

You've likely heard the phrase, "You are what you eat." It applies spiritually too. As we consume the Word of God and its truth about who and Whose we are, equipping rises within us to walk in the ways of love and life. We've been given a new nature in Christ and will act out of what we believe about ourselves.

2 Corinthians 5:17 says, "Therefore, if anyone is in Christ, the new creation has come: The old has gone, the new is here!" We must believe we are made new. We are His, and out of that unity and intimacy, we behave in ways that are true to the renewed self we've been born into.

However, that alone doesn't guarantee our victory over sin and its consequences—we still have choices to make.

Free will fueled by grace and relationship

Having been recreated and established in our new identity, we still can choose to act in ways that don't honor the Spirit in us. The Holy Spirit is our Guide into righteous living. He becomes our internal GPS that directs us in the way we should go.

He also comforts us if we take a wrong turn and reroutes us, so our destination produces life rather than death. Still, we are the ones who decide if we will walk in the direction He's leading us in.

Our free will is described in Deuteronomy 30:15–16 (AMP; brackets in the original), "Listen closely, I have set before you today life and prosperity (good), and death and adversity (evil); in that I command you today to love the LORD your God, to walk [that is, to live each and every day] in His ways and to keep His commandments and His statutes and His judgments (precepts), so that you will live and multiply, and that the LORD your God will bless you in the land which you are entering to possess."

As God leads us by His Spirit, we get to choose whether we'll submit to His life-producing and loving Lordship or succumb to the deception the enemy has for us. Daily we face this decision—will we allow Jesus to be Lord by believing what He said about us and then walking in step with Him in that truth? His grace will be there for us as we do.

There's a mandate for every believer to know what the best course of action is in every situation, according to the ways of Christ—which is love. Beyond knowing is doing, and that's what the believer is commissioned and empowered to do by God's grace. Following the Spirit and His ways is the mark of a true disciple.

It's ironic that in giving ourselves completely unto Him, we gain true freedom. Inviting Him in, not only as Savior but also as Lord, requires humility and obedience. The result of complete surrender is the ability to keep demonic attacks and the enemy's lies from gaining influence in our lives.

There's a surrender to the leading of the Holy Spirit that is asked of us if we desire to live as Jesus did. Galatians 5:16 says, "So I say, walk by the Spirit, and you will not gratify the desires of the flesh." If we choose to be influenced by the Spirit, fueled by identity and

God's grace, the benefits are endless. His Holy Spirit in us is our continual saving grace.

Love-filled decisions, inspired by the Holy Spirit, invite health into every area of our lives. We've been given every tool needed to live such a life, through our relationship to God, as His righteous children.

Once we're established in righteousness and our worth is secured, it affects our behavior. As unconditionally loved children, we no longer have anything to be ashamed of and behave out of what we believe is true about us.

Psalm 103:12 (NLT) says, "He has removed our sins as far from us as the east is from the west." This promise reminds us we can live in the complete delight of the Father. We must be fully rooted in the love of God. A firm foundation regarding God's nature toward His children is essential in order to receive from Him.

Heart Connection

1. Read the lyrics to "Lord, I Need You" – Matt Maher.[3] I've provided a link for you here: https://www.azlyrics.com/lyrics/mattmaher/lordineedyou.html.

   Are any phrases resonating with you? If so, ask the Holy Spirit what He wants to communicate to you. In a journal, jot down what you hear.

2. Listen to the song "Lord, I Need You."[4] I've provided a YouTube link for you here: https://youtu.be/LuvfMDhTyMA.

   What else is the Holy Spirit speaking to your heart? Be sure to write it down.

3. Have you struggled with guilt and condemnation in your life? The enemy is swift to remind you of your weaknesses. I encourage you to shift your focus during those times.

   Meditate on 2 Corinthians 12:9, "My grace is sufficient for you, for my power is made perfect in weakness." Write down what the Holy Spirit reveals to you about this Scripture. Ask Him for other Scriptures you can memorize that will help you battle the enemy's lies when they come.

4. God's grace covers us and empowers us to do all things. What specific areas in your life are in need of God's grace? List them out as a prayer offering to God. When His grace comes through for you, thank God and write the testimony down.

5. Have you ever considered your oneness with God? How does that knowledge change what you think about yourself and what you're able to accomplish in Him?

Chapter 12

Our Father

Freedom from disease and dysfunction is ours as we reach for the righteous garment God provides through Christ. His righteousness allocated to us brings us into a life-giving relationship with God as our Father.

As a good Catholic girl, I knew the Lord's prayer by heart. However, it wasn't until I heard a message from a favorite Bible teacher of mine, Katherine Ruonala, when a revelation came about how Jesus wants us to address God in prayer and what that means for us.

"This, then, is how you should pray: '*Our Father* in heaven,' " (Matthew 6:9). Jesus teaches us how to pray by inviting us to call upon *our* Father. He was saying, His Father and your Father are one and the same.

After Christ's resurrection, Mary Magdalene goes to Jesus' tomb and finds it empty. He comes to her and says, "Mary, don't hold on to me now, for I haven't yet ascended to God, my Father. And he's not only my Father and God, *but now he's your Father and your God!* Now *go to my brothers* and tell them what I've told you, that *I am ascending to my Father—and your Father, to my God—and your God!*" (John 20:17 TPT).

Our unity with Christ brings us straight into the loving arms of our Papa, who provides for us and delivers us from evil.

Your identity as a child of God and what that means

Often people believe God can help and heal but that perhaps He isn't willing. The nature of parents is to guard their children—to protect them, provide for them, and teach them to stay out of harm's way. It's no different with our Heavenly Father. In fact, it's better!

Matthew 7:11 (NLT) says, "So if you sinful people know how to give good gifts to your children, how much more will your heavenly Father give good gifts to those who ask him."

Obviously, we want our own children to thrive and be well. How much more does a sacrificial and loving God, whose justice toward sin was already satisfied in Himself, want the same and even more for His children?

We need to remind ourselves we are children of God! "The Spirit you received does not make you slaves, so that you live in fear again; rather, the Spirit you received brought about your adoption to sonship. And by him we cry, '*Abba*, Father' " (Romans 8:15; italics in the original).

God has chosen us to be His very own children!

Revelation of God's nature as a good Father

Our relationship with God, as our Father, has the potential to bring healing as we discover His true nature. Often, we equate

God's nature as a Father with experiences we've had with our earthly fathers.

That may be good or bad, depending on the kind of father we had. An essential part of our healing journey is the ability to separate who our earthly fathers were from who our Heavenly Father is. We must lay aside what we think we know based on our human experience and encounter truth through simple trust in the One who made us and desires to Divinely Father us.

The Holy Spirit loves to reveal what our Father is really like—and He's a good one! He's our Heavenly Father, and Heavenly means just that—He is Heavenly! God is altogether wonderful and kind! We know this because Jesus represents Father God to us in the life He led. Colossians 2:9 (NLT) says, "For in Christ lives all the fullness of God in a human body." The heart and will of God the Father are evident through the life of Jesus that we read about in the Gospels. John 5:19c (NLT) says, "Whatever the Father does, the Son also does."

Mark Greenwood, a pastor from Glory City Church in Australia, says the following in explaining God's nature, "If it doesn't look like the Son, don't call it the Father."[1] He talks about Jesus being the exact representation of God.

The Bible is clear on the subject; Jesus mirrors God Himself. Hebrews 1:3 (NLT) states, "The Son radiates God's own glory and expresses the very character of God." Philip, one of the apostles, asked for Jesus to show him the Father. Jesus replies in John 14:9b, "Anyone who has seen me has seen the Father."

Jesus healed everyone who came to Him. We must know God is a good Father who is for us and for our healing, just as Jesus displayed throughout His ministry. Our identity as sons and daughters of a Father who does good, and heals us, is our portion.

When we know the kind of Father we have and His heart toward us, we begin to understand our value apart from what we do, and we can then receive all the benefits we have as His children. Jesus tells us we enter into the Kingdom of God when we come like a little child. Matthew 18:3 reads, "And he said: 'Truly I tell you, unless you change and become like little children, you will never enter the kingdom of heaven.'"

The Kingdom of Heaven comes with the benefits of righteousness, peace, and joy in the Holy Spirit (Romans 14:17). Our ability to receive from our Father—and what citizenship in His Kingdom offers—has a lot to do with how we see ourselves in God's eyes.

Revelation of our worth to God brings healing

Value in the marketplace is determined by what someone is willing to pay for something. Think about all Jesus gave up and suffered to purchase you back to the Father—you're that valuable! The revelatory knowledge of God's love for us and our Christ bought position with the Father, as dearly loved children, sets us up to reign in life.

It begins with a real relationship that culminates into healing as we learn our worth to the very One who sent His Son to suffer and die in our stead. Being firmly planted as the child of a good Father who makes us worthy to receive every promise is vital.

If that concept doesn't fit well with you, then there's some work to do! Without that revelation, your healing will likely not come. Think about when someone has gotten you a gift. Do you question why they got it for you and insist they shouldn't have? Are you sheepish about accepting it?

Do you say, "You didn't have to do that!"

Well, of course, they didn't *have* to do it. Out of love, they wanted to!

Suppose you're having lunch with a friend, and they reach for the bill to pay for your meal. What's your response? If you believe you don't deserve the blessing, you're likely to deny the gift.

"Oh no, that's okay, please don't."

In the same way, you'll struggle to receive all Jesus died and resurrected to give you if you believe and behave as though you're not worthy of His gifts—or if you think you must earn them.

Imagine, as a parent, if I refuse my son dinner if he doesn't do well on his school exam that day. What if my child went skateboarding and having slid off the path he got hurt, and I did nothing? What kind of parent would choose to look away and refuse to bandage up their child's wounds because they left the house without cleaning their room as they'd been asked to?

Most parents provide for their children's needs automatically. It isn't based on merit but rather unconditional love. It is no mistake God calls Himself a Father, and we are His highly valued children. We must know who we are, in relation to God, to receive what He has for us.

Coming to God like a child to receive from Him

Have you ever heard of a child refusing a brand-new toy or a trip to the ice-cream shop for their favorite treat?

Jesus gives us a key to receiving the goodness of God in our lives, "And he said: 'Truly I tell you, unless you change and *become like little children*, you will never enter the kingdom of heaven'" (Matthew 18:3). This Scripture describes our born-again experience and invites us to ponder what little children are like so we can enter into the fullness of God's Kingdom for us.

Children don't strive—they ask for what they need

Little children don't try to earn their keep. They don't question their parents' provision; they simply receive. They know they're loved. They aren't concerned with their behavior or question whether they're measuring up. Children begin in purity and innocence.

If we are to become like little children, we're to stand in our place of righteousness in Christ—in His purity and innocence. In this place of rest and freedom from striving, there is no fear of judgment or punishment. It allows us to freely receive, based on nothing more than God's kindness and not our own behavior.

Children ask for their needs to be met—sometimes at the top of their lungs! I'm not recommending we behave childishly, but we can learn much about the value children carry based on nothing more than their ability to ask and receive freely.

Matthew 7:7 encourages us, "Ask and it will be given to you; seek and you will find; knock and the door will be opened to you."

Children know their value and don't judge or compare

Little children don't question their worth. They're as real as can be, authentic, and unashamed with how God created them. Unlimited in their freedom to simply be who they are—they run, skip, dance, and sing. Often, they'll invite an audience!

"Look, Mom! Watch what I can do!"

They don't struggle with a poor image of themselves. They aren't concerned, in the least, about what they look like. Have you ever seen a toddler pinch the rolls on their tummy or thighs in disgust? They haven't yet been engulfed in a world system that has them questioning, comparing, and distorting their value.

2 Corinthians 10:12 advises against comparison, "We do not dare to classify or compare ourselves with some who commend themselves. When they measure themselves by themselves and compare themselves with themselves, they are not wise."

The only measurement we're to compare ourselves with is the standard of being in Christ. Since we are in Him, we're completely perfect in God's eyes, just as Christ is. We are to see ourselves in His fullness as a precious son or daughter of God.

1 Corinthians 4:3 says, "I care very little if I am judged by you or by any human court; indeed, I do not even judge myself." God saves us from self-judgment as we look at ourselves through the mirror of Jesus Christ.

Overanalyzing and judging ourselves happens, little by little, as we grow older and are inundated in a world filled with comparison and unnecessary expectations. We're also tempted to judge others. Young children, in their purity, don't have judgment written on their hearts. To judge another is based on an old nature we've been redeemed from in Christ.

Children don't judge others because they don't sow judgment upon themselves. Hosea 10:12 says, "Sow righteousness for yourselves, reap the fruit of unfailing love, and break up your unplowed ground; for it is time to seek the LORD, until he comes and showers his righteousness on you."

Having a clear picture of who we are, as pure and righteous in Christ, allows us to love others in the same way—without judgment. 2 Corinthians 5:16 (NKJV) says, "Therefore, from now on, we regard no one according to the flesh." As we look at others through a spiritual lens, we'll see them as God sees them. Children, who've yet to be tainted by sin, naturally do this.

Children are dependent and trusting

Little children are dependent. We notice the beginnings of independence as infants enter toddlerhood, and it continues to grow from there—as it should. Yet, our complete dependency on the Holy Spirit for daily living is a principle we must learn to cultivate.

We tend to think we can do things on our own. Jesus says, "I am the vine; you are the branches. If you remain in me and I in you, you will bear much fruit; *apart from me you can do nothing*" (John 15:5).

Do you remember as a small child saying, "I do it myself, Momma!" Then haphazardly trying to do something beyond your capability? Next thing you know, breakfast is in your hair and your pants are on backward.

Our dependency on Christ for our righteousness, and His help and guidance for abundant daily living, must continually be at the forefront of our minds. The Holy Spirit is available to us every time we turn to Him. As I lift my hands in worship, I often think that I'm communicating to God, "Up, Daddy." It's a reminder that He's my source and comfort in all things.

We can also glean from the ability of a little child to freely trust— to believe. They are completely dependent on their parents for provision. A child doesn't worry about where their next meal is coming from. They don't toil over anything, really. Perhaps it's the reason children laugh four-hundred times a day, while adults laugh only fifteen![2]

Jesus speaks to us about not worrying in Matthew 6:25–34. He tells us not to worry about our lives in any way and promises our needs will be met by our Father. "Look at the birds of the air; *they do not sow or reap or store away in barns*, and yet your *heavenly Father* feeds them. Are you not much more valuable than they?" (Matthew 6:26). This Scripture talks about a bird's provision and how it isn't based on their own efforts, and it applies more so to God's children—you and me!

Those who run frantically after provision instead of trusting God don't know Him as their Father. Matthew 6:32–34 says, "For the pagans run after all these things, and *your heavenly Father* knows that you need them. But seek first his kingdom and his righteousness, and all these things will be given to you as well. Therefore do not worry about tomorrow, for tomorrow will worry about itself. Each day has enough trouble of its own."

Children are quick to forgive

Children naturally live by the Kingdom principle of forgiveness. To forgive someone requires letting go. We can allow God to carry away the burden of holding something against another person.

Harboring unforgiveness in our hearts is like lugging around a heavy suitcase without wheels. Matthew 6:14 (AMPC; brackets in the original) instructs us, "For if you forgive people their trespasses [their reckless and willful sins, leaving them, *letting them go*, and giving up resentment], your heavenly Father will also forgive you."

Promises are attached to forgiving those who have harmed us. We gain release from the emotional baggage of bitterness and resentment. Those destructive emotions, left unresolved, can ultimately manifest in our bodies and cause illness.

God feels strongly about the topic of forgiveness. In fact, forgiveness isn't optional. We generally think of promises from the Bible in a positive light. When it comes to choosing unforgiveness over mercy, a negative promise naturally results. We won't be forgiven.

The parable of the unmerciful servant in Matthew 18 shares with us incredible insight regarding the responsible party for such consequences. Hint: it isn't God.

In any kingdom, there are laws that govern. God Himself lives under these laws, and so does Satan. Jesus teaches us about some key Kingdom principles as He tells us the story of a king who settles accounts with his servants.

One of his servants is unable to pay the debt he owes. Upon hearing all he has is to be sold to repay what he owes, including his wife and children, he pleads for his master to be patient with him a while longer. The servant asks for more time to pay his debt off. The king chooses mercy and decides to cancel what he owes entirely.

Soon after, the servant finds a person who is indebted to him. He owes him a small amount in comparison to what he previously owed the king. Still, he harshly insists on being paid back the debt. "He grabbed him and began to choke him. 'Pay back what you owe me!' he demanded" (Matthew 18:28b).

The servant refuses to give mercy, even at the heels of the king forgiving him of a much larger debt. When the king is told about how the servant refused to show mercy, as it had been given to him, a reckoning comes. Galatians 6:7 says, "Do not be deceived: God cannot be mocked. A man reaps what he sows."

The servant finds himself confronted with the Kingdom principles of giving mercy and reaping what you sow. It's the same thing most of us were taught in kindergarten. Matthew 7:12 (NLT) instructs, "Do to others whatever you would like them to do to you. This is the essence of all that is taught in the law and the prophets." By his own doing, the servant allows the enemy to have a say in his life by partnering with his ways instead of God's principles.

The parable continues with the king upholding the laws of the land with the following questioning and consequence, " 'Shouldn't you have had mercy on your fellow servant just as I had on you?' In anger his master handed him over to the jailers to be tortured, until he should pay back all he owed" (Matthew 18:33–34).

This scenario reveals who is ultimately responsible for the torture that ensues when unforgiveness overshadows Kingdom mercy. The jailer represents Satan who's allowed access into our lives when we partner with his ways over God's ways. We choose our fate through unforgiveness, which God requires, and Satan runs off with us chained in his cuffs.

The good news is that we hold the key to the chains that bind us. We can choose to forgive others when they owe us what is comparatively insignificant when we look at how Jesus continually forgives us and the price He paid for our sins.

It's interesting to note this parable is told right after Peter asks Jesus how many times he's supposed to offer forgiveness to those who repeatedly sin against him. He wonders if seven times is enough. "Jesus answered, 'I tell you, not seven times, but seventy-seven times' " (Matthew 18:22). Jesus' response draws Peter away from a particular number as a standard and to the same limit God has in forgiving man—to which there is no limit![3]

Forgiveness is what brought victory over the kingdom of darkness at the cross. It can do the same in our own lives if we choose to walk according to Jesus' instructions. To behave differently is to partner with torture and the one who delights in keeping us in its grip—the devil.

When the temptation comes to hold on to unforgiveness, we can choose to release ourselves from the chains through God's Kingdom principles of grace and mercy. Satan only has power over us if we allow it. We get to choose which kingdom we will take part in. Choose to be like a child who forgives and forgets quickly, then watch the Kingdom of God manifest in your life.

God wants to show Himself as a Father, who is strong on your behalf. Intimacy with Him, through the Holy Spirit, allows an open door for Father God to speak into your life. The result is the prospering of your soul and body.

Heart Connection

1. Read the lyrics to "Good Good Father" – Chris Tomlin.[4] I've provided a link for you here: https://www.azlyrics.com/lyrics/christomlin/goodgoodfather.html.

    Are any phrases resonating with you? If so, ask the Holy Spirit what He wants to communicate to you. In a journal, jot down what you hear.

2. Listen to the song "Good Good Father."[5] I've provided a YouTube link for you here: https://www.youtube.com/watch?v=iBmwwwiHrOk.

    What else is the Holy Spirit speaking to your heart? Be sure to write it down.

3. When you think about the nature of God, what comes to mind? If you're familiar with Scripture, do you see God as Jesus was in the Gospels? How does it make you feel to know God and Jesus have the same nature?

4. How was/is your relationship with your earthy father? Do you find yourself thinking God's character is like his? Ask God how He is the same or different in nature to your earthly father.

5. Do you have children? Consider how you are as a parent. What qualities do you share with Father God in relating with your children? What areas can you improve on? Bring them to the Holy Spirit for counsel.

    If you don't have children, consider someone special in your life. How do you show unconditional love toward them? What are some areas in your relationship you can ask the Holy Spirit to help you with?

Part 3
Prospering in Soul & Body

Chapter 13

Intimacy with Our Healing God

I remember the day when, at nineteen, I received the diagnosis of lupus.

It was a long drive from the doctor's office to home—and distance wasn't the issue. Time seemed to stand still as I recalled all that was said.

I was going to have to start another medication in addition to the thyroid pill I'd been given weeks earlier for the fatigue I was experiencing. Not even out of my teens—I couldn't understand how I was suddenly on two daily medications. Especially since I'd recently met Jesus and knew He could heal me supernaturally.

Nevertheless, my battle with illness began. I went from one medication to another, often producing only temporary relief. Not to mention side effects—ungodly side effects! Medication isn't wrong—I'm still taking some. In fact, because of the kidney transplant, I'm on medicine that suppresses my immune system so my body doesn't reject my donor's kidney.

This isn't about one or the other—medication or God. I believe God gives scientists the wisdom for many of the treatments we have today. Luke, one of the Gospel writers and the author of the Book of Acts, was a doctor himself—that alone speaks volumes. Having said that, I do believe if we aren't getting to the root cause of disease, many prescriptions are more like Band-Aids rather than solutions.

Getting under my own bandages took time. I needed intimacy with God to receive the truth and healing He had for me.

I was a believer; why was I still sick?

I was new to Christianity at the time of the lupus diagnosis. Only weeks in, really. I'd read the Gospels and the other books of the New Testament. Many of the Psalms and Proverbs were part of my daily reading as well. As a result, I believed in God's healing. With every fiber in my being, even the ones that were being attacked, I was certain God could heal me in an instant.

I'd even experienced a touch from God—His tangible Presence. I knew He was real; I knew He was pure love! He had spoken to me directly through tongues in my baptism experience and told me about my bright future; chronic illness was never on the list.

Even if my personal experience with the Lord was subjective, I knew the Word of God wasn't. Jesus healed everyone who came to Him. Matthew 15:30 (NLT) says, "A vast crowd brought to him people who were lame, blind, crippled, those who couldn't speak, and many others. They laid them before Jesus, and *he healed them all.*"

All!

I was confused. Why wasn't healing happening for me? I knew the Word of God was concrete on the issue. Psalm 103:1–3 told me so, "Praise the Lord, my soul; all my inmost being, praise his holy name. Praise the Lord, my soul, and forget not *all* his benefits— who forgives *all* your sins *and* heals *all* your diseases."

There was that *all* again. Didn't I fit into the *all* category? I noticed the *and* in that Scripture too. Based on God's Word, forgiveness and healing were a package deal. Salvation was my benefit in Christ, and so was healing—both were included!

Jesus is our Savior *and* Healer

The Word of God was crystal clear on the subject of healing, just as it had been regarding salvation. The prophet Isaiah spoke of the coming Savior of the world in Isaiah 53:4–5 (AMPC; brackets and italics in the original), "Surely He has borne our griefs (sicknesses, weaknesses, and distresses) and carried our sorrows *and* pains [of punishment], yet we [ignorantly] considered Him stricken, smitten, and afflicted by God [as if with leprosy]. But He was wounded for our transgressions, He was bruised for our guilt *and* iniquities; the chastisement [needful to obtain] peace *and* well-being for us was upon Him, and with the stripes [that wounded] Him we are healed *and* made whole."

There it was in black and white again! Jesus' role as Healer in spirit, soul, and body was spoken long before He walked a single step on the earth's soil. Jesus didn't suffer a gruesome death and victoriously resurrect only to pay the price for my sins. He came to rescue me from sin *and* take away every disease.

The Gospels exemplify Christ as The Healer, "And you know that God anointed Jesus of Nazareth with the Holy Spirit and with power. Then Jesus went around doing good and healing *all* who were oppressed by the devil, for God was with him" (Acts 10:38 NLT).

God heals because it's who He is—Healer

I've heard people say that lack of faith keeps a person from being healed. It's condemning to hear such a thing, and it's completely incongruent with the nature of God.

If healing were based on a person's ability to believe, they'd have something to boast about when they got healed. They might be tempted to think it happened based on their belief rather than on God's goodness. The Bible says in 1 Corinthians 1:29 (NKJV), "That no flesh should glory in His presence."

All we receive from the Lord is based on His good nature and not our own ability to produce it. It's that way with salvation, and it's also true of healing. Romans 11:36 says, "For from him and through him and for him are all things. To him be the glory forever! Amen."

My own faith isn't the deciding factor concerning receiving the promises God has outlined in Scripture. It is Spirit-infused faith, imparted to me by the Holy Spirit, that brings about His promises. My confidence comes from the faith God first gives me about who He is.

A personal revelation about God's nature is the place we can rest in and receive from. James 1:17 says, "Every good and perfect gift is from above, coming down from *the Father* of the heavenly lights, who does not change like shifting shadows." He is the gift giver and extends kindness out of His unchanging loving nature as a Father who heals.

One of the names God uses to describe Himself is recorded in Exodus 15:26 (ESV), "For I am the LORD, your healer." The original Hebrew names for "LORD your healer" are *Yahweh-Rapha* or *Jehovah-Rapha*. God's name means Healer. It's not just what He does; it's who He is.

Incidentally, *Rapha* in Hebrew also means "to mend, cure, repair thoroughly, make whole."[1] It encompasses God's restoration of creation into a right relationship with Him and includes ridding the body of physical and emotional ailments.

Hearing from God brings faith and healing

Information for the mind without revelation within the heart produces little. Romans 10:17 (NLT) says, "So faith comes from hearing, that is, hearing the Good News about Christ." The Greek word used for hearing in this passage is *akoé*, defined as inner (spiritual) hearing that goes along with receiving faith from God.[2]

Discerning God's voice initiates faith. Healing and faith have less to do with knowledge and more to do with hearing from the Healer Himself. Knowing God's nature and experiencing Him is what brings healing. It's His Presence we need. We're not to put our faith in faith itself but rather in the One who gives it.

I was immersed in what God said about healing in His written Word, and I believed it to be absolute truth. I knew a ton of Scripture concerning God's desire to heal, many by heart. Every miraculous encounter Jesus had with the sick and downtrodden, I'd read about them. Beyond having a lot of head knowledge, I even had a supernatural experience with God as my Healer!

I'd experienced healing before; why not now?

"Hey, what is that?" I asked.

I leaned in aimlessly, trying to figure out where the noise was coming from. I swerved my head from side to side, waiting for my friend's reply.

"What's what?"

How could she not hear that awful sound?

I hastily opened the front door and told her, "It's like the sound of a garbage truck in continual reverse."

The bustle of leaves in the wind from the robust cottonwood trees greeted me first. I next heard a young couple carrying on a conversation from afar. The beeping stopped.

Relieved the noise was finally gone, I closed the door only to discover the grating sound had returned.

I asked again, "Ok, seriously, you can't hear that?"

Fully annoyed at this point, I tried to explain it anew.

"It sounds like the mini tractor at Costco as it backs up to stock a shelf. You know, the one that's always blocking the exact item you need to get to?"

She came back with the same blank stare as before—claiming not to hear the sound that was so blatantly ringing!

I found out later the ringing was due to a condition called tinnitus. This was early on before the lupus diagnosis.

Tinnitus is temporarily cured in the presence of other sounds.[3] That's why I couldn't hear the ringing when I swung wide my apartment door. Nature acted like a white noise machine, disguising the continuous sound that was apparently only present between my two ears in the quiet.

I looked at the doctor while pressing against both ears.

"Ugh, I can't stand this noise! Please, make it stop!"

His reply offered zero hope.

"I'm sorry, there's no cure."

It was the first time I'd heard that darkened phrase and wouldn't be the last. I was later told the same regarding lupus. For now, I was dealing with this persistent ringing and thought to pray. I hadn't yet been born-again. Still, I had enough mustard seed faith to ask God for healing.

"God, heal me, please?"

My prayer was that simple, question mark and all. Jesus said the amount of faith required to command a mountain to relocate was the same size as a mustard seed (Matthew 17:20). Have you seen a mustard seed? They are one to two millimeters in size— that's tiny![4]

The following morning, with no earthly reason to have had a different outcome than what I'd been experiencing for the last few weeks, I was completely healed!

Not a single beep—I sat up in the bliss of sweet silence.

God came through, even before I was a believer! What was the problem now that I actually believed He was my Healer? Why was lupus holding on for so long? God alone had the answers I needed to come out from under sickness and disease. Clearly, I was missing something. I intended to find out what it was.

Wisdom and revelation were the missing links

My entire Christian walk was marked with a love for the Word of God, but I was missing a key element. Once I found it, everything changed and healing followed.

Though I knew a lot of Scripture, the promises they held remained elusive to me. Things like peace of mind and physical healing for my body were only written words on a page and not tangible realities in my life, even though I knew them to be true—in theory.

As much as I read, recited, and believed, its manifestation in my experience was gravely lacking. It wasn't until I began praying just as the Apostle Paul did for the church in Ephesus when things finally started to shift, "I keep asking that the God of our Lord Jesus Christ, the glorious Father, may give you the *Spirit of wisdom and revelation, so that you may know him better*" (Ephesians 1:17).

My agreement to see that same prayer answered in my own life changed everything. As I read Scripture, I began to invite the Holy Spirit to come and make His Word alive in me. In humility, I finally asked for *His* wisdom and revelation and that I would know Him better. The real Him, not what I thought He was like based on my past experiences with life apart from Him.

I bought a brand-new Bible, leather cover and all. I had John 8:32 imprinted on the front, in no less than gold lettering, "Then you will know the truth, and the truth will set you free." Back then, I didn't fully know the implications behind those Words.

I delved into time with the Father and soon realized that truth has a capital T. It's a Person—it's God, it's Jesus, it's the Holy Spirit. I needed to be encountered by Truth Himself. His Presence would rest on me, and healing would come as a result.

God's Presence brought truth and healing

I prepared our place of meeting. With my warming blanket on high, candles lit, and heaps of hazelnut creamed coffee at my comfortable reach, I intentionally sat with God in quiet surrender.

Day after day, I asked of my Maker, *"God, I want heart revelation, not just head knowledge. Let me truly know and fully experience what you're saying to me personally and awaken all you want for me to live in and enjoy."*

The King of kings snuggled up with me in my "Jesus chair"— I'd given the oversized accent chair in my living room, where I sat to read my Bible, that name long ago. Now, it held even more meaning because "the name that is above every name," as Jesus is referred to in Philippians 2:9, was in it with me! Who knew Jesus wanted His own invite?

I could feel His delight and excitement over my invitation. I basked in the warmth of His smile and imagined His chin on my shoulder as we both looked at the pages set before us. I was eager to engage. He was just as thrilled to enlighten my heart and have its contents unveiled so He could bring truth for my healing.

It reminded me of times when I purchased the perfect gift for someone. I couldn't wait for them to unwrap it! I'd hand-picked a special treasure specific to them. Sharing in their pleasure as they first set their eyes on it was my absolute delight. Nothing pleased me more, and I knew my Savior felt the same. Especially since His nail-scarred hands paid the price so He could turn the gift-filled pages of Scripture—right alongside me.

The Word and Spirit work together to bring healing

There was nothing wrong with my accumulated knowledge of the Bible. In fact, without it, there wouldn't have been anything inside my spirit for the Spirit of Wisdom and Revelation (the Holy Spirit) to breathe on and bring life out of.

It never occurred to me there was another essential element needed to gain all God had written down for me to possess. Jesus said in John 4:24 (NLT), "For God is Spirit, so those who worship him must worship in spirit and in truth." Information alone would not do!

Once I discovered welcoming in His Presence brought truth and revelation to the Words I was reading, only then did authentic growth and healing begin. I read it unlike I'd been accustomed to before—now, I asked questions.

Psalm 27:4 (ESV) says, "One thing have I asked of the LORD, that will I seek after: that I may dwell in the house of the LORD all the days of my life, to gaze upon the beauty of the LORD and to *inquire in his temple*." A royal invitation awaited my opening, "Your Majesty, King Jesus, requests the pleasure of your company as you behold His beauty; bring questions, no gifts, please."

Experiencing God and inquiring of Him was my salvation for eternity but also for the here and now. Psalm 27:13 assured me, "I remain confident of this: I will see the goodness of the LORD in the land of the living."

I began to understand the true nature of God and who I was to Him through the answers the Holy Spirit gave me. As I made a conscious decision to relate to the Word of God, through the Spirit of God, changes began to happen in my mind, will, emotions, and physical body.

Immanuel, a Hebrew name meaning "God with us,"[5] was my new guest of honor through humble invitation. His acceptance was always sure—He painfully died to come.

Although my healing journey began when I accepted Christ in my life, it seemed to have progressed at a turtle's pace. Now, the wholeness I desired was being fueled by the work of the Word *and* Spirit. The dynamic duo worked together, revealing truth and instruction for life, and with that came ultimate healing.

Restoration of all that ailed me was finally at my fingertips with each turning page—in His Presence. Jesus says in John 14:26, "But the Advocate, the Holy Spirit, whom the Father will send in my name, will teach you all things and will remind you of everything I have said to you."

The Holy Spirit brings to our remembrance the Word of God. His Presence and power bring to light who He is for us in every circumstance in our lives. In that, we learn what we mean to Him. He also helps us determine the direction we're to take and guards our way.

Psalm 37:23–24 says, "The LORD makes firm the steps of the one who delights in him; though he may stumble, he will not fall, for the LORD upholds him with his hand." He directs our steps and becomes our remedy should we veer from the path that leads to life.

Light always overcomes darkness. Imagine a tiny match in a large and unlit room, all attention is immediately drawn to its small flicker. It's the illumination of the Word of God, by the Holy Spirit, that sets us on paths out of the darkness and into God's light and freedom.

In John 8:12a, Jesus says of Himself, "I am the light of the world. Whoever follows me will never walk in darkness, but will have the light of life." Much of my life was marked with grappling through the trenches of darkness; disease constantly beckoned at my door.

Would my turning to the One, who was light Himself, in this new way—both in Word and Spirit—bring about the abundant life I desperately desired?

We need the *Logos* and *Rhema* Word of God to heal

There are two Greek words the Bible uses to describe the Word of God. *Logos* encompasses the entire communication of God's Word.[6] For simplicity's sake, consider it as generally referring to the written Word of God. That's the way in which I engaged with the Lord before discovering the *Rhema* Word of God, which is a specific Word from the Spirit.[7]

A *Rhema* can be viewed as a sub-component of the *Logos*.[8] It becomes a spoken Word of God, to our own heart, based on God's written Word. John 4:23–24 describes God's intention for us, "Yet a time is coming and has now come when the true worshipers will worship the Father in the Spirit and in truth, for they are the kind of worshipers the Father seeks. God is spirit, and his worshipers must worship in the Spirit and in truth."

The *Logos* Word of God and the *Rhema* spoken Word of God intertwine to produce life. I needed both, and this discovery brought about the renewal and restoration of my spirit, soul, and body. Jesus says in John 6:63b, "The words I have spoken to you— they are full of the Spirit and life." The very breath of God brings life to His Word.

2 Timothy 3:16–17 says, "All Scripture is God-breathed and is useful for teaching, rebuking, correcting and training in righteousness, so that the servant of God may be thoroughly equipped for every good work."

The work God calls us to is continually opposed by the enemy. Disease and disorder of every kind are the devil's weapons of choice. His defeat is sure as we utilize the victory God has given us through His Word and the Holy Spirit who reveals it.

The Word of God becomes a powerful response to attacks from the enemy. It muzzles and thwarts every lie Satan attempts to perpetuate in our lives. It's the very reason the Word of God is described as a sword, "Take the helmet of salvation and the sword of the Spirit, which is the word of God" (Ephesians 6:17). The Word of God in this particular Scripture is referring to a *Rhema*. Our weapon against enemy attack is in having a personal Word spoken to us.

As I sought the Holy Spirit for His personal Words to me, the darkness in my life began to diminish. Intimacy with the Father brought light to all that was ailing me, in soul and body.

Conversations with God give us the personal battle strategies and revelations we need to irradicate chronic illness and any other attack from the enemy against us. If you haven't already, invite the Holy Spirit to speak into your life. He can't wait to share what's in His heart for you! Pray this with me:

Father God, thank you for speaking to me through the Holy Spirit living in me. I'm grateful you've given me a partner in life to show me your love, give me your counsel, and heal me in every way. I need to hear from you! I invite you to speak to my heart, help me to see you, and hear from you. I don't want to miss a single Heavenly kiss you have for me! Teach me to follow your ways in the Kingdom. In Jesus' name, I pray. Amen.

Heart Connection

1. Read the lyrics to "Jesus, You're Beautiful" – Jon Thurlow.[9] I've provided a link for you here: http://www.songlyrics.com/jon-thurlow/jesus-you-re-beautiful-lyrics/.

   Are any phrases resonating with you? If so, ask the Holy Spirit what He wants to communicate to you. In a journal, jot down what you hear.

2. Listen to the song "Jesus, You're Beautiful."[10] I've provided a YouTube link for you here: https://youtu.be/_FdaESoZKvg.

   What else is the Holy Spirit speaking to your heart? Be sure to write it down.

3. When you study the Word of God, do you invite the Holy Spirit to bring His wisdom and revelation? I encourage you to do so and watch as the Lord reveals His Truth directly to your heart!

4. Do you have a desire to cultivate a deeper relationship with the Holy Spirit?

   Ask the Holy Spirit to reveal Himself throughout your day, watch and listen for the messages He has for you. I call these encounters with God Heavenly kisses. When you get them, be sure to thank the Lord for His kindness and write down what you saw or heard.

5. Do you need battle strategies for a particular situation in your life right now? Have you struggled with the same issue for far too long?

   Ask the Holy Spirit to reveal the personal plan He has for you and then implement His instructions. Be sure to ask for His help, remember *Immanuel* is with you!

Chapter 14

Hearing from the Healer

My health was a mess, my mind besieged, and my emotions awry.

God, please take away this pain, silence the vexing thoughts, and free me from fear. Jesus, help!

I rambled on in my journals without pause.

How, then, could He respond? A silent moment was all the Lord needed.

I didn't realize He was interested in a partnership. He was dying to have a real relationship with me—He had already died for it.

I prayed so many times for His miraculous rescue when all along He sent His Holy Spirit to speak to my heart, to build me up in what He had already done on my behalf, and to show me who and Whose I was.

I was loved. I was filled with the Holy Spirit and made righteous. I belonged to God!

Truth wanted to be my constant Companion. Out of that, I could receive all God had for me and behave in ways that were congruent with that revelation.

Any earthly relationship requires communication to survive, let alone thrive. For the longest time, I didn't know it was the same with God.

Communication is dual. What if someone only spoke at you and never listened for a response? If a long list of questions, concerns, complaints, and requests were set before you, I imagine you'd feel confounded when the person never took time to listen to what you had to say on the matter. It might cause you to wonder why someone would bother to ask for help in the first place. What would the point be?

If we behaved in the same way with our boss, co-workers, friends, and family, there would be a serious cause for concern. Yet, this is how I carried on with God—until I learned prayer is not a monologue.

It's rather an exchange, a conversation between God and His child. It's supposed to be a vibrant dialogue between God and His friend. As we encounter God in this relational way, we begin to truly understand and take in all Jesus redeemed for us. This propels us into a place of healing in every area of our lives.

Rewards come as we dialogue with the Holy Spirit

Have you ever been around someone who talks incessantly? You can barely get a word in edgewise! Disguised in their massive and often dramatic monologues are needs. They may just seek to be heard, but often they're looking for advice. The problem is, they aren't listening!

Appropriately named, monologue comes from the Greek words *monos* "alone" and *legein* "to speak."[1] As a chosen daughter in Christ, one that had been made His very own, God wanted to turn my monologue into a dialogue with Him. He was the One who had the answers to the sickness in my soul needing to be healed.

I wonder if our anatomy has a message hidden within it from God. Philosopher Epictetus penned these words long ago, "We have two ears and one mouth so we can listen twice as much as we speak."[2]

He wasn't the only one to coin phrases along these lines. American playwright Eugene O'Neill poetically wrote, "God gave us mouths that close and ears that don't...that should tell us something."[3]

God was willing to hear all about my needs, desires, and longings. What good was it if I didn't stop to take in His comfort or listen for His direction?

We go to God because He is love, and we desire to be immersed in all that He is. He is worthy of our attention and adoration, apart from all else. It's His Presence we seek, and yet the Lord tells us in Hebrews 11:6b (NLT), "Anyone who wants to come to him must believe that God exists and that he *rewards* those who sincerely seek him."

In all His goodness, the outcome of personal relationship and inquiring of God are the rewards of life and wholeness. He gives out of His goodness, and He is a rewarder of those who put faith in who He is for them. We get to partake in His marvelous grandeur as we bask in His Presence and listen for the Words of life He has available for us.

Psalm 16:11 says, "You make known to me the path of life; you will fill me with joy in your presence, with eternal pleasures at your right hand."

I was accustomed to giving God long speeches about my cares and woes. It helped, to a degree, in that I wasn't keeping everything bottled up inside. God was gracious enough to always listen.

The problem was, without waiting for a response, I never came away with a strategy—especially when it came to overcoming the things that plagued my mind and my physical body. He had a battle plan for me against the enemy of my soul—all I needed to do was to listen. God's invitation for me to inquire of Him still stood. My questions were welcome in His Presence.

Even Jesus had questions for God. He inquired in Matthew 27:46 (italics in the original), at what was likely the height of His suffering on the cross, "About three in the afternoon Jesus cried out in a loud voice, '*Eli, Eli, lema sabachthani?*' (which means 'My God, my God, why have you forsaken me?')."

Once I tuned in to God's Presence and began asking questions—with an expectation to receive answers—they came! The heart healing I was so desperate for ultimately produced physical healing as well.

The ways God speaks to us are countless

As I began to listen, I found the Holy Spirit spoke in various ways, beautifully and uniquely. The Bible is our greatest resource in discovering how God speaks to His people. *Rhema* Words from God bring answers, hope, and life to any situation we face.

I believe God is speaking far more than we're listening. He's always offering us His direction. Jesus says in John 10:27, "My sheep listen to my voice; I know them, and they follow me." Once I realized that it was perfectly normal to hear from God, and a conversation was something He desired as well, I began to pray for it.

Lord, let me hear you today. I don't want to miss a single Heavenly kiss.

I've been blessed in hearing from God through His Word, of course, but I've also encountered God through thoughts that bubbled up in my heart. I've experienced Him through life circumstances where His nature remained consistent. He's often brought wisdom to me through another person or used dreams to give me direction.

He has used songs to impart truth to me. I've received messages from God while watching a movie or when I've been out and about running my everyday errands. Everywhere I am, there He is to speak! I've felt His Presence in worship and have seen visions within my Spirit as He's spoken to me through a picture in my mind. The ways God speaks to us are limitless!

I discovered in my quest for conversations with God that to hear from Him, I should not strive for it. Everything in the Kingdom of God comes to us from a place of rest and humility.

God invites us to a life of humility

There was much to weed out in the garden of my wounded heart, and yet God was calling me to a place of rest. In a lifestyle of intimacy with the Holy Spirit, there's a reprieve from laboring for all Jesus has already purchased on the cross to freely give us.

It's in this place of trust, rest, and listening where restoration and healing flourish. Psalm 46:10 says, "Be still, and know that I am God; I will be exalted among the nations, I will be exalted in the earth."

In the original Hebrew language, "be still" means to let go—to surrender.[4] It implies such a degree of trust in our good Father that we're able to allow ourselves to become weak, so He can show Himself to be strong on our behalf. The truth is, we are already weak. It's in that humble realization and acknowledgment when God's strength comes to our rescue. 2 Corinthians 12:10b says, "For when I am weak, then I am strong."

Humility is a superpower. Jesus says, "Take my yoke upon you and learn from me, for I am gentle and humble in heart, and you will find rest for your souls" (Matthew 11:29). The help we need comes to us as we ask and listen for His direction.

A simple prayer will do: *God, I don't know what to do, but you do. I trust you are always for me. I believe you will guide me. Help me to follow you.*

Life with God is similar to a dance. If both partners take the lead, there will be a struggle—and perhaps the trampling of a toe or two! Surrendering to follow the leading of the very One who desires to carry you in the dance of life brings your soul rest and refreshment. 1 Peter 5:6 (NLT) says, "So humble yourselves under the mighty power of God, and at the right time he will lift you up in honor."

As we turn from our own wobbly efforts to save ourselves and look to the One who directs us to serene paths with Him, we will lack nothing. Psalm 23:1–3 (ESV) says, "The LORD is my shepherd; I shall not want. He makes me lie down in green pastures. He leads me beside still waters. He restores my soul. He leads me in paths of righteousness for his name's sake."

Healing flows naturally from a place of humble surrender and into the arms of the One who gave it all to hold us securely in His love, power, and provision.

I hear the Father asking, "May *I* have this dance?"

The Holy Spirit has answers for us

As we make room for God's voice in our lives, we acquire wholeness in spirit, soul, and body. In any area of life where we lack ease, the Holy Spirit holds the answer for us to overcome. Whether it be our struggle against sin and dysfunction, the climb out from a health crisis, or the healing of a broken heart into wholeness, God makes Himself available to us.

All that attempts to beset us, our Savior valiantly comes to comfort, heal, and empower us to move forward. If we quiet ourselves enough to hear, the Holy Spirit speaks; it's that simple.

The answers to coming out from under all that ailed me were at His feet. I had access to the mind of God through the Holy Spirit living in me. 1 Corinthians 2:12–16 (ESV) says, "Now we have received not the spirit of the world, but the Spirit who is from God, that we might understand the things freely given us by God. And we impart this in words not taught by human wisdom but taught by the Spirit, interpreting spiritual truths to those who are spiritual. The natural person does not accept the things of the Spirit of God, for they are folly to him, and he is not able to understand them because they are spiritually discerned. The spiritual person judges all things, but is himself to be judged by no one. For who has understood the mind of the Lord so as to instruct him? *But we have the mind of Christ.*"

The provision of Christ's perspective regarding every moment of my life was being made accessible to me as I sought the Holy Spirit. The One who knew the scenes of my life, before any of them came to pass, had the answers on how to heal the hurts that came from them.

It's as though God had already watched the entire movie of my life, from beginning to end. All that brought joy—He rejoiced in it with me. All that brought hurt and harm—He saw and cared about what happened. He was willing to bring restoration and even recompense through my union with Him.

The Father knew why I did the things I did. He had direct access to the roots in my soul that caused pesky weeds to continually grow in my garden of life. With the slightest look in my direction, the Almighty could pluck them out solid—I was certain of it, but He wanted more than that.

He was interested in a dance partner.

The cycle of defeat in so many areas of my life was finally subject to change as I sought the leadership of the only One who had the answers my soul craved. Many Christians faithfully pray, without knowing God loves to respond and will speak to them. The One who knows all things, because He created all things, loves to direct His children.

Psalm 32:8 gives us a glimpse of the Father's heart regarding this aspect of His giving nature, "I will instruct you and teach you in the way you should go; I will counsel you with my loving eye on you." Almighty God is the ultimate strategist! He knows the way; He *is* the way, "Jesus answered, "I am the way and the truth and the life. No one comes to the Father except through me" (John 14:6).

Will we stop long enough to listen?

What happens at your house when visitors are coming? The Bible tells us about two sisters, one named Mary and the other, Martha. The Son of God was in town and coming over! Martha was busy with preparations for the visit, while carefree Mary "sat at the Lord's feet *listening* to what he said" (Luke 10:39).

I feel like Martha gets a bad rap sometimes. Someone had to shove everything in the closet, clean the bathroom, and make dinner! Still, when Martha complains to Jesus about her sister's hippie-like ways, He responds rather surprisingly to any type A personality out there.

"'Martha, Martha,' the Lord answered, 'you are worried and upset about many things, but few things are needed—indeed only one. Mary has chosen what is better, and it will not be taken away from her' " (Luke 10:41–42).

Martha was distracted by work while Mary listened (Luke 10:40). The distinction between the two is simple: while one labored, the other chose to rest. Mary sat at Jesus' feet and indulged in all He had to offer her—don't you wonder what He said to her? The Bible doesn't offer us that information, but I do know this—when I've taken time to sit at the Lord's feet to listen, He's continually spoken His unrelenting love over me, and it was exactly what I needed.

When I first started listening for God's voice, I remember receiving the same Words from Him over and over. They were foundational—I needed to know them before anything else could take root; I needed to know I was fully accepted and loved.

Recognizing God's voice through thoughts

The Spirit continually impressed this thought in my mind, "Mimi, I love you."

When I'd ask what was on His heart for me that particular day, His response came flooding in, "You!" Doesn't that make you smile?

Those Words aren't just for me, they're for all of God's children.

We can know it's God putting thoughts in our mind when they're congruent with His nature, when they line up with Scripture, and by what the thoughts produce in our lives. My first yearnings as a new believer were to walk in the fruit of the Spirit, "But the Holy Spirit produces this kind of fruit in our lives: love, joy, peace, patience, kindness, goodness, faithfulness, gentleness, and self-control" (Galatians 5:22–23a NLT).

This Scripture continued to be a lifeline for me. Not only had the fruit of the Spirit become attainable to me since they'd been deposited within my heart by the Holy Spirit, but they were also a guide in determining the origin of thoughts that came to my mind. I learned any thoughts that didn't encompass the fruit of the Spirit were not from God.

The thought, "Mimi, I love you," which I felt God was speaking to me, was in line with the first fruit mentioned: love. Scripture should always be our baseline in determining whether we're hearing God's voice, our own thoughts, or the enemy's lies.

I knew God's Words for me were from Him because they were in perfect alignment with the fruit of the Spirit and other Scriptures. Jeremiah 31:3 says, "The LORD appeared to us in the past, saying:

'I have loved you with an everlasting love; I have drawn you with unfailing kindness.' "

Psalm 139 speaks about the intimate nature in which God knows us. Everything lays bare before Him. Every choice we've made, every single moment of our lives—He's aware of each one. "If I go up to heaven, you are there; if I go down to the grave, you are there. If I ride the wings of the morning, if I dwell by the farthest oceans, even there your hand will guide me, and your strength will support me" (Psalm 139:8–10 NLT).

The good, the bad, and the ugly—He knows all about it, and yet the measure of His precious thoughts about us remain and are countless. "How precious are your thoughts about me, O God. They cannot be numbered! I can't even count them; they outnumber the grains of sand! And when I wake up, you are still with me!" (Psalm 139:17–18 NLT). When God spoke to me, through my thoughts, that I was on His mind—I knew it was from Him and that it was true according to His Word.

The other surety came from what the thoughts produced in my life. It gave me peace and joy to hear God loved me and was thinking of me—it fell in line with the fruit of the Spirit! I could be certain God was speaking to me.

Maturity comes through God's gentle correction

God's thoughts toward us are always good. That doesn't mean He won't bring correction when needed—every good parent does— and God is a good Dad. Proverbs 3:12 (NLT) says, "For the LORD corrects those he loves, just as a father corrects a child in whom he delights."

God desires we attain the fullness of the inheritance Christ purchased for us. Often, that requires growth. We may endure some growing pains as we mature, but the results are well worth the temporary pain.

It's God's kind nature to direct us in the way we should go. God leads us to repentance out of His kindness (Romans 2:4). We must always remember His discipline originates and comes from a place of unrelenting love.

Maturity is asked of us from a Father who desires we receive all He has for us. In our relationship with God, we stay child-like, but that's not to be confused with childishness.

The heart of God is to protect His children, and being mature in Him is our safeguard against harm. Sons and daughters enjoy the privileges that come with loving discipline and the result it produces. Romans 8:17 says, "Now if we are children, then we are heirs—heirs of God and co-heirs with Christ, if indeed we share in his sufferings in order that we may also share in his glory."

Recognizing God's love through situations

As I grew in my confidence regarding God's love for me, there were certainly times of correction and maturing that took place— but they didn't come until He first established His unrelenting love within my heart. I had to know when discipline and correction came that it wasn't punishment but rather a safeguard from harm.

As I continued to spend time with the Lord, He built on the foundation of His love for me by teaching me about my identity as His handpicked daughter. I found myself in situations where God blessed me, in spite of my behavior.

When I knew I hadn't behaved as I should have, perhaps through showing impatience or anger toward another person, I'd tell God I was sorry. His response was to carry on with me as though it never happened!

My past taught me to fear mistakes and that not behaving perfectly in line with expectations was unacceptable. I wasn't used to this level of mercy and this kind of unconditional love.

Hebrews 8:12 says, "For I will forgive their wickedness and will remember their sins no more." There were even times when an extra blessing would come my way at the heels of willful disobedience!

How could this be?

The blessings that came weren't based on anything I'd earned or accomplished. In fact, I deserved the very opposite, but it seemed as though my behavior wasn't a factor. He taught me through life's situations that His goodness toward me was based on my identity and righteousness in Christ alone. It was that revelation that helped me to stand in the worth and value He died to give me.

As a result, I was finally able to receive from His loving hand. A personal connection with my Father, based on nothing more than His good nature and not my performance, opened up a realm where healing could flow to me freely.

He had Words of wisdom and gentle guidance every time I turned to Him. My ears were finally open to His love and direction because fear had been driven out (1 John 4:8).

Sincere love comes from the Author of it: God. It's a gift given to us through the Holy Spirit, and it's what heals our broken hearts. It helps us overcome the dysfunction of unhealthy behavior and even addiction in our lives. His unconditional love enables us to love other people properly, which has a healing effect on our own souls.

The beauty is that God gives us His love first (1 John 4:19). Only then are we able to operate in love toward others and even ourselves. You can only give to someone what you already have.

Receiving from God equips us to give

I live in a quaint suburban neighborhood tucked on the outskirts of a larger city. Even though the grocery store is only a few miles down the road, neighbors often rely on each other for unexpected missing recipe items.

Suppose my neighbor is in the middle of baking cookies. The flour, butter, eggs, and butterscotch chips have already made their way into the mixing bowl. She digs in her pantry to find she's shy of a cup of sugar.

Since we're friends, and it's quicker and easier to make a trip down the sidewalk than driving to the store, she comes knocking on my door with a measuring cup in hand.

"Hey, Mimi, can I please get a cup of sugar from you?"

Of course, my answer would be yes, but I could only give it to her if I actually had some sugar on hand. I can only give away what I already have.

We're incapable of producing "sugar" without the Spirit's work in our lives. He is the Author of love, and He gives it to us, so we can then give it to others.

The Spirit in us is the very Presence of God and affords to us all He is. The pure nature of God's love has already been deposited within us through the Holy Spirit. As we listen to God's voice over all others, His love is cultivated and can be drawn out.

The question is, will we first knock on His door for the sugar we need? If we know Him as our loving Father and faithful Friend, surely, we will.

Spending time with my Best Friend

Certain people come into your life that show themselves to be true friends. They're the ones you can be completely yourself around, and they faithfully show up for you in time of need.

Indifferent to a clean house, or even the makeup you usually wear around those you aren't as close to, they simply pull up a chair and are there. With a messy kitchen and bare face in full view, you feel free to share about your victories—and also your mishaps and failures.

Experience has told you they won't shame or degrade you. You're safe to be vulnerable because you know they've been faithful to be by your side, no matter what.

A good friend will rejoice with you over the good and lift you out of the pit of disappointment you may be carrying over the not so good. A really good friend will listen carefully and may even offer a perspective you haven't thought of yourself.

As I offered the Lord His own kitchen chair, sharing from my unrestrained heart with full expectation to receive love, comfort, and reply—He became my Best Friend. Just as He had surely been for His disciples. John 15:15 says, "I no longer call you servants, because a servant does not know his master's business. Instead, I have called you friends, for everything that I learned from my Father I have made known to you."

I was thrilled to have the Holy Spirit as my new constant Companion. I was learning how to lean in and receive from Him. All good friendships are reciprocal, so I wanted to be a good friend to Him and others too.

Much like a garden, if we tend to it, it will flourish and produce. Beauty and nourishment are the results of diligently giving Jesus our time and attention. Relationship with man began in a garden, and Jesus brings us back to its bliss, as we allow Him to be the Master Gardener of our hearts.

Like a tender friend, I found the Holy Spirit was continually on my side. As I listened, He became my Advocate and Helper just as John 14:16 (NASB) describes, "I will ask the Father, and He will give you another Helper, so that He may be with you forever." He knows us better than we know ourselves and helps us examine things from His perspective, an all-knowing and Heavenly one.

He knows all about the areas we might keep hidden from even our closest friends, and He loves us still.

God spoke to me about the enemy of my soul

As God's love became more established in my heart, I began to look to Him for guidance in every area of my life. He revealed to me that although He was my good Father and faithful Friend, I had an enemy that needed to be dealt with.

Just as God showed me His thoughts toward me, He made me aware there was a battle raging in my mind over them. If I were to lend my ears to God's thoughts—freedom and life would follow.

Philippians 4:8 says, "Finally, brothers and sisters, whatever is true, whatever is noble, whatever is right, whatever is pure, whatever is lovely, whatever is admirable—if anything is excellent or praiseworthy—think about such things." The devil's thoughts counter this kind of thinking and always oppose the fruit of the Spirit as defined in Galatians 5:22.

Through a dream, God showed me how the enemy works and revealed how to deal with Him. Dreams in the night are another way we can receive revelation and hear from our Healer.

Heart Connection

1. Read the lyrics to "You Know Me Better" – Stars Go Dim.[5] I've provided a link for you here: https://www.azlyrics.com/lyrics/starsgodim/youknowmebetter.html.

    Are any phrases resonating with you? If so, ask the Holy Spirit what He wants to communicate to you. In a journal, jot down what you hear.

2. Listen to the song "You Know Me Better."[6] I've provided a YouTube link for you here: https://youtu.be/pOGlS5yz3zs.

    What else is the Holy Spirit speaking to your heart? Be sure to write it down.

3. Have you experienced God's unconditional love for you? There is nothing that will bring more healing to your soul! Think about some ways God has shown you His unchanging love and express to Him your gratitude.

    Receiving God's love is an ever-increasing experience. Ask the Holy Spirit to show you more of His love and write your experiences down as He does.

4. We've all heard of the power of positive thinking. I believe the revelation of God's thoughts toward us have a greater impact beyond our own ability to think positively. God's truth spoken to us by the Holy Spirit brings healing and permanent transformation.

    Ask the Holy Spirit what some of God's thoughts are toward you. Write down what you hear and meditate on the truths you've received. If they're consistent with God's Word, you can be certain they are coming straight from His heart to yours. Enjoy!

5. Think about a person in your life that you consider a friend. What are some of the characteristics of a good friendship? Do you see the Holy Spirit as your Friend? If so, thank Him now for His friendship.

    If you have yet to recognize the Holy Spirit as your Best Friend, ask Him to make you aware of when He's fulfilling this role in your life. As He does, be sure to thank Him and remember to be His friend too. He loves to hear from you!

Chapter 15

Revelation through a Dream

The devil acts like a pesky tick, attempting to suck the life out of God's children through accusation and lies. Before my relationship grew with my Savior, through listening to Holy Spirit revelation, I relied on my own strength to deal with the torment of the enemy.

I was ignorant of his ways and the relentless attacks he hurled at me. I accepted the thoughts he perpetrated into my mind as being my own. Back then, I didn't know any better.

I had struggled for years, believing I was unattractive and that my body was hideous. I was blindingly consumed with every degrading thought the enemy fed me. Until God gave me a *Rhema* Word through a dream—with strategies to defeat him.

Dreams are another avenue God uses to speak to us. He used them to direct countless people in the Bible, and He still does today.

Let me tell you about the dream God gave me that taught me how to defeat the enemy. I believe it will help you too!

The revelatory dream that set me free

Encased in a dark hallway, I noticed everything was in shades of black and white. My surroundings were hazy and gray like in an old movie. Someone stood by my side. I felt the comfort of their Presence, even though they spoke no Words. I didn't look to see Who it was; my attention was focused elsewhere.

High above my head were four disproportionately huge and antagonistic faces—the eyes of each zeroed in on me. Each one morphed into another as they took turns speaking. The sounds coming from their mouths were muffled, and their words unintelligible.

The images reminded me of a scene from the *Wizard of Oz* when Dorothy and the crew finally come before the Great and Powerful Oz. Unlike the cowardly lion, I had no fear. I was fortified by the Presence next to me.

I pointed my finger at the faces and asserted, "Bow down, in Jesus' name!"

I kept repeating the same words.

As I spoke, the giants got quieter. Partly from my demand that they bow down—but that wasn't the only reason. It was their ploy to draw me in closer, and I fell for it. I leaned in to try to hear what they were saying. As I did, my once robust command for them to bow down became faint, and my pointed finger and arm weakened in strength.

In a moment, rescue came! Above the giant faces, I saw the Holy Spirit fluttering down in the form of a dove. I smiled as if I'd seen the arrival of a long-awaited friend who unexpectedly came for a visit.

I began to clap and exclaim, "Thank you Holy Spirit, thank you!"

Rejoicing danced from my lips, and in a flash, the faces that once drew my attention vanished! Instead, I saw an opening in the sky in the shape of a perfect square. Within were clouds wrapped around the bluest sky with birds soaring, boasting vibrant rainbow colors on their wings.

Contrary to the rest of the dream, within this square glimpse of Heaven were incredibly defined and crisp colors. The hues were unlike any I'd seen on earth. I felt incredible peace and desired to stay in that moment forever. Then, as quick as the snap of a finger—I woke up.

I asked the Lord what He wanted to teach me through the dream. As I prayed, God revealed some powerful spiritual weapons Christ provides for us through our relationship with Him.

Power through Presence, the Word, and His name

God immediately brought two Scriptures to my remembrance. He told me I was wise to His Word in Luke 10:18, "I saw Satan fall like lightning from heaven." I recognized the faces speaking at me were the enemy. The moment the Holy Spirit entered the picture, they fell out of the sky.

The other Scripture the Lord highlighted was Philippians 2:9–11, "Therefore God exalted him to the highest place and gave him *the name that is above every name, that at the name of Jesus every knee should bow*, in heaven and on earth and under the earth, and every tongue acknowledge that Jesus Christ is Lord, to the glory of God the Father."

When I told Satan's varied faces to "bow down, in Jesus' name," I was using my authority in Christ. Using the name of Jesus is powerful against the enemy's work; it's above any other name, and the enemy must submit to it.

The Lord continued to encourage me and gave me more truth. He spoke to my heart, "The enemy holds power only if you choose to give it to him." It was significant in the dream that the faces didn't have bodies. They have nowhere to go unless we empower them to walk into our lives. We have the authority of God's Word, the name of Jesus, and the Presence of the Holy Spirit—to silence them.

If I give my attention to the devil and his words, leaning in to hear his lies, only then will I be weakened. In the dream, I positioned myself closer to the devil's lying tongue instead of away from him. As I did, the strength of my voice and hand against him began to falter.

When the devil speaks to us, we can use the Word of God and our authority in the name of Jesus. As we do, we will see him fall like lightning from the sky. In giving our attention to the Holy Spirit and away from Satan's lies, we maintain the power Christ has already given us.

God showed me how the Holy Spirit's Presence was with me the entire time. He was the Friend that stood at my side in the dream, and He later showed Himself to me in the form of a dove. He also lives in me—He was the One who breathed life into the Scriptures I knew, allowing me to use them in battle.

I felt God's Fatherly pride as He continued, "The Holy Spirit will always come to your rescue." The Holy Spirit reminds us of God's Word in every situation we face. Proverbs 3:6 (ESV) says, "In all your ways acknowledge him, and he will make straight your paths."

As the ultimate strategist, with all knowledge and wisdom, the Holy Spirit brings to our remembrance what we need to fight every battle. "But the Advocate, the Holy Spirit, whom the Father will send in my name, will teach you all things and remind you of everything I have said to you" (John 14:26). His Presence is our wisdom, peace, comfort, and encouragement. The Holy Spirit always shows us the way.

His paths are full of life, with a richness only He can give. We take hold of it as we hear God's voice through the Spirit and walk in the direction He leads us in.

Isaiah 63:13–14 (NASB) tells us about how the Spirit of God was with Moses and what His Presence produced in the life of God's people. "Who led them through the depths? Like the horse in the wilderness, they did not stumble; Like the cattle which go down to the valley, The Spirit of the LORD gave them rest. So You led Your people, To make for Yourself a glorious name." The Holy Spirit gives us rest, regardless of our circumstances—that's powerful. In it, He brings glory to His name—that's worship!

Presence through worship and thanksgiving

Worship is a weapon. God is glorified through children who listen for His direction and do what He says. The natural consequence of following God's ways is victory, and it leads us into a place of thanksgiving and worship as we acknowledge what He's done for us.

As we choose to put our attention on Him and follow His instructions, putting Him over and above any trial we face, He is glorified. Placing our trust in God brings Him honor.

The Lord reminded me that I began to rejoice when I saw the Holy Spirit in my dream. It was at that moment when the Heavens opened. Our worship gives Heaven an opportunity to come into the scenes of our lives. The enemy voices and their corresponding faces vanished once I saw the Holy Spirit and thanked Him.

God inhabits the praises of His people (Psalm 22:3), and where He is, all darkness must flee. Psalm 18:3 (ESV) says, "I call upon the LORD, who is worthy to be praised, and I am saved from my enemies." Giving God the praise He deserves is the avenue into His Presence—and where He is, there is protection.

Psalm 91:1 (ESV) reassures us, "He who dwells in the shelter of the Most High will abide in the shadow of the Almighty." The entire Psalm depicts the all-encompassing care and protection of our faithful God. It's the awareness of who God is for us that instinctively provokes thanksgiving from our hearts to His.

No unrest or sickness can lay hold of us as we remain in Him and thank Him for the provision He offers. Isaiah 26:3 (NLT) says, "You will keep in perfect peace all who trust in you, all whose thoughts are fixed on you!"

Amid emotional turmoil or physical pain, there's a place in God's Presence where angst in soul or body is overshadowed. As we worship God through trust and keeping our thoughts on Him, we're hidden beneath His wings from harm.

Rainbows signify God's promise of hope and protection. There are over thirty-three verses about rainbows in the Bible, and they point to God's covenant of mercy toward His people.[1] There's no doubt the birds with the rainbow-colored wings in my dream were a message from God to me about His Presence and faithfulness.

Where He is, everything dark is overcome with His very own light. John 8:12 (ESV) says, "Again Jesus spoke to them, saying, 'I am the light of the world. Whoever follows me will not walk in darkness, but will have the light of life.' " Life comes to us by being enfolded in the arms of Christ. Our healing process takes place as we rest in God's goodness and Presence—and worship and thanksgiving are the avenues to get us there.

The distinction between worship and thanksgiving

Worship and thanksgiving are distinct, and yet they intertwine. When we worship, we look to God for who He is and appreciate His unchanging character. We worship Him for His attributes.

Lord, you are Faithful and kind, a valiant Warrior who works on behalf of those who love you. Thank you!

When we give thanks, we posture our hearts in appreciation for what God has already done in our lives.

Thank you, God, for answering my prayer today. I know it was you that softened my friend's heart, so we could communicate and resolve our differences.

In any relationship, it's common courtesy to thank the person that has blessed us in some way. Just as we appreciate acts of kindness from other people, we honor our Heavenly Father by thanking Him for His goodness toward us as well.

Thanking God for what He will do in the future keeps us in a place of rest and peace. Philippians 4:6 says, "Do not be anxious about anything, but in every situation, by prayer and petition, *with thanksgiving*, present your requests to God."

We can choose faith over anxiety and give God thanks, in advance, for what we believe God will do. Our trust in Him is based on His good nature and what He has revealed is available to us in His Word.

Thank you, God. I believe you're working in my life and giving me a strategy to get out of debt.

As we ask of Him, we give thanks as though it were already a done deal. It's that process that brings us into peace. The passage in Philippians continues in verse 7, "And the peace of God, which *transcends all understanding, will guard your hearts and your minds* in Christ Jesus."

As we give thanks in our asking, His peace comes even when we don't understand why a situation is happening or when and how it will be resolved. It's a position of power, and it gives God honor.

Laying aside our own agenda and thought processes, to rest in the only One who can help us overcome every torment the evil one hurls at us is our privilege as the beloved children of God.

Whether the enemy's attack of the day is through feelings that have gone awry, frustrations that have taken their toll, or physical ailments that threaten to keep us from the life we desire to live in fullness—worship and thanksgiving overcome the chaos.

Unfavorable circumstances desire to draw our attention toward them instead of God. We can choose whether we will worship God or the issues in our lives. Accepting God's invitation to meditate on Him, rather than our problems, is a true act of worship.

Worship is a natural consequence of knowing God

Worship isn't simply a song we sing, although that can be what it tangibly looks like. Rather, it's a choice to believe God by placing His goodness over and above the situations we face in our lives. This is only possible once we know Him. It's impossible to trust someone you don't know. The natural result of knowing God is to trust Him and faith in Him leads to worship. Trusting in God and worship go hand in hand.

If we desire to worship God, then we must become familiar with Him and His ways. The good news is, God wants to be known. He gives us His Word so we can get to know His ways. He gives us His Spirit to bring us into the truth about Him and who He desires to be for us.

As we develop a relationship with God, He begins to share with us about who He is and who we are to Him. This empowers us to walk tall in our true identity as unconditionally loved children of God. As His children under His care, our relationship to Him brings us into a place of safety and security.

His love toward us and His provision through Christ provokes heartfelt worship and thanksgiving. You can't help but love Him when you know how much He loves and cares for you.

From what I'd read in the Bible, I had long known worship and thanksgiving were powerful weapons against the enemy. The walls of Jericho coming down in Joshua 6:4–5 are only one example, but the Lord gave me my own unforgettable revelation through the dream.

I witnessed firsthand the opening of the Heavens as I began to give thanks in seeing the Holy Spirit. The scene, with its dynamic colors, will forever be etched in my mind. These are the type of *Rhema* encounters with God that solidify truth within our hearts; we need personal revelation!

Revelation for direction and victory

Encounters with God are a prize waiting for those who worship Him. They provide an experience that solidifies what the Word of God has been telling us all along. They teach us to gather for ourselves truths that last because they have become a part of us.

God may also give you revelation and direction through a warning dream. Joseph is only one example of someone who experienced this type of dream in the Bible. Matthew 2:12 (ESV) says, "And being warned in a dream not to return to Herod, they departed to their own country by another way."

God gives us instructions on how to thwart the enemy as we turn our attention to Him. Revelation from God requires time in reflection with the Holy Spirit. His instructions bring freedom through the truth He gives us so that we can have prosperous lives.

I've only shared one dream and the takeaways God gave me as He spoke to my heart. Dreams are a wonderful way God uses to bring direction on how to live victoriously in our daily lives. There's an open invitation for anyone who chooses to listen to God in this personal and unique way. Remember to apply the fruit of the Spirit in determining who is speaking. If a dream brings life-giving direction and healing, you can be certain it's the work of the Lord.

Be sure to ask for dreams in prayer. Matthew 7:7 says, "Ask and it will be given to you; seek and you will find; knock and the door will be opened to you."

It's amazing to know the God of the entire universe speaks to us, even in the night hours. My prayer is that we will listen to Him, day and night! Psalm 16:7 says, "I will praise the LORD, who counsels me; even at night my heart instructs me."

Let's pray together now:

Father God, thank you that you've provided everything we need through our relationship with you. Help us to know you better so we can trust you in every circumstance we face. Speak to us, Lord, the strategies we need in order to overcome. Thank you that your truth brings freedom! Open up our dream life and communicate to us through it. We want to hear from you through every avenue you have for us. We look to your Word, your Presence, and the name of Jesus for our wisdom, rest, peace, and power. Thank you for giving us worship as a weapon. You are worthy of praise! In Jesus' name, I pray. Amen!

Heart Connection

1. Read the lyrics to "I'm Listening" – Chris McClarney.[2] I've provided a link for you here: https://www.azlyrics.com/lyrics/ chrismcclarney/imlistening.html.

   Are any phrases resonating with you? If so, ask the Holy Spirit what He wants to communicate to you. In a journal, jot down what you hear.

2. Listen to the song "I'm Listening."[3] I've provided a YouTube link for you here: https://www.youtube.com/watch?v=nT8iKdwbKdU.

   What else is the Holy Spirit speaking to your heart? Be sure to write it down.

3. Has God spoken to you in a dream? If so, what did you learn? Apply the principles you were given.

   If you aren't sure if God has spoken to you in a dream, I'd like to encourage you to consider that He likely has! Perhaps you didn't realize it was from Him? Ask the Holy Spirit to speak to you in the night hours and pray for the interpretation.

4. The enemy is always trying to have a voice in our lives. Our safeguard against Him is through our relationship with Christ.

   Ask the Holy Spirit to reveal to you some thoughts you've been bombarded with that are from the enemy. The next time the enemy speaks a lie to you, what measures can you take to combat it?

5. Worship and thanksgiving are powerful weapons we've been given. Take some time now to worship God for His love and good nature toward you. Thank Him for what He has already done in your life and for what you know He will do in the future.

   Be encouraged as you read Ephesians 3:20–21, "Now to him who is able to do immeasurably more than all we ask or imagine, according to his power that is at work within us, to him be glory in the church and in Christ Jesus throughout all generations, forever and ever! Amen."

Chapter 16

Freedom in Truth

As I began listening to the Holy Spirit, day and night, inner healing started to take place, and my body reaped the benefits as well. I found what was going on in my physical body was a manifestation of things I believed about myself.

Beliefs, whether true or not, become true for us if we believe them. They cement themselves in our souls and require God's truth and healing.

The amount of responsibility I grew up with, coupled with my parents' cultural influence regarding discipline and other ideals, caused turmoil in my soul. Expectations were high, and even a small amount of disobedience wasn't tolerated. As a result, I grew up fearful.

False beliefs were created in my soul. I wasn't free to express how I really felt about things. My experience told me I didn't have a voice and that I couldn't be flawed. Essentially, I couldn't be me.

I based my value on what I did and felt accepted only when my behavior was in line with the expectations I was under. Although my parents loved me, deep down I always felt I had to behave perfectly; when I didn't—shame entered in.

Shame was later solidified through a series of poor choices I made. Those choices were also a clear reflection of what I falsely believed about myself; I was invisible and needed to gain worth through whatever means.

Freedom from shame through love and identity

Shame says there is something wrong with me—instead of there is something wrong with what I did. Separating who we are from what we do is essential if we're to gain victory over the debilitating effect shame has on our souls. Joyce Meyer says, "We have to know the difference in our who and our do. Who we are in Christ is different than what we do."[1] My performance became linked with who I was. God never intended for me to live a life of conditional love for myself.

When Jesus is asked what the greatest commandment is, He answers in Mark 12:30–31, " 'Love the Lord your God with all your heart and with all your soul and with all your mind and with all your strength.' The second is this: 'Love your neighbor *as yourself.*' There is no commandment greater than these."

As a believer, I was being called not only to honor others and esteem them but to do the same for myself. Shame doesn't allow for that.

Jesus made me a perfect creation in Christ, regardless of my behavior. I *knew* I was loved. I had all the right theology, but it didn't have me. It had yet to become a *Rhema* Word, spoken to my heart on a personal level.

In living without this heart revelation, shame had me turning to food and overeating for comfort. Relentless dieting seemed to be my only option, later igniting bulimia and overexercising as part of the vicious cycle. Without God's Truth, I lived in perpetual dysfunction.

My value was connected to my physical appearance. I was consumed with thoughts about how I looked. I thought perfection would somehow satisfy the deep longing of my soul to be seen, heard, and accepted. My deepest desire was to have a voice and to feel worthy. On my own, I couldn't get there—but I certainly tried.

The devil had me convinced that if I looked a certain way, worthiness would come. Instead, shame took over all the more. My struggles became my identity; shameful was who I became.

Self-hatred over sin and not behaving perfectly, even when it came to my diet, ate me from the inside out. It kept me from being whole. Food, a perfect body, and the acceptance of others was never the solution.

Only Jesus' unconditional love could set me free. That revelation, straight to my heart and not just in my mind, was what I needed. It would require stepping into my righteousness in Christ and working through some of my belief systems.

My first step to wholeness was certainly through salvation in Christ, but it was clear my soul needed more tending to. As I became intimately acquainted with the voice of the Holy Spirit, inner healing came with it and began to drive out the ungodly forces of fear and shame that had attacked me for so long.

Unresolved emotions began to surface, and as they did, the Lord healed them with His comfort and truth. The result was ultimately the manifest healing of my physical body as well.

Getting to the root of our problems

When there's a struggle in our lives that remains, even after accepting our perfection in Christ, we must ask the Holy Spirit to help us see the root of the issue. Often, lies have implanted in our souls and have grown to bring a harvest of pain. When we don't deal with the pain, it deals with us. Our actions are proof of that reality.

Our struggles can be connected to the past or current life circumstances we don't want to face; this is also known as denial. We fill ourselves with distractions rather than dealing with the pain. In our attempt to self-medicate, we hide from the truth. We end up landing in the grip of unhealthy behavior and even addiction. It's visible in our struggles with food, weight, drugs, alcohol, overspending, and health issues. The list is endless.

God has more for us!

Anything we do in excess serves as a sign of something deeper going on, vying for our attention. The denial in our lives needs to be addressed as God gently exposes the truth about what's really going on inside of us that's being expressed through destructive eating behavior or whatever our self-medication of choice is.

We emerge from its deadly side effects with help from the Holy Spirit.

Freedom through Holy Spirit truth

Exposing the lies we believe about ourselves, and even other people, helps us go from denial to freedom. The lies we believe are rooted in our past, the things that have been done to us or maybe not done for us. Over time, they become strongholds in our minds. Left to ourselves, we react to them in unhealthy ways.

Our salvation comes in that we are not left on our own to overcome. We've been given the power to live in victory over every lie through our intimate relationship with the Holy Spirit. 2 Corinthians 10:4 says, "The weapons we fight with are not the weapons of the world. On the contrary, they have divine power to demolish strongholds."

God uses the Word and His Spirit to change our beliefs and faulty ways of thinking to bring healing. God instructs us in Romans 12:2a saying, "Do not conform to the pattern of this world, but *be transformed by the renewing of your mind.*"

The lies we've learned to believe about ourselves must be replaced with the truth about who God says we are. Our true identity must rise out of the ashes. It's the Holy Spirit who works on our behalf to get us there.

1 Corinthians 2:10–11 (AMP; brackets and italics in the original) says, "For God has unveiled them *and* revealed *them* to us through the [Holy] Spirit; for the Spirit searches all things [diligently], even [sounding and measuring] the [profound] depths of God [the divine counsels and things far beyond human understanding]. For what person knows the thoughts and motives of a man except the man's spirit within him? So also no one knows the *thoughts* of God except the Spirit of God."

Through our relationship with the Holy Spirit, truth is revealed to us. His truth dispels every false message we've received throughout our lives about who we are and who God is for us.

The lies are what fuel our destructive behavior patterns. The unresolved wounds in our souls have created belief systems contrary to the Word of God, and it shows through our actions. Our personal discovery into these areas of our hearts take Holy Spirit revelation—and that takes relationship.

I needed the truth of the Word of God to bubble up from my renewed spirit, travel to my mind, and overtake my soul. The veil over my eyes regarding who I was in Christ needed to be lifted. My secure identity had to be established so I could receive God's goodness in my life. I needed His light to shine in and reveal what He was really like, His nature.

I needed to know who He was for me personally—my safe Father and caring Friend. I didn't realize those key truths in the beginning.

In fact, I didn't know them for the longest time, even as a believer.

I tried to stand on the Words in Scripture without the Word Himself. His Presence was required for my healing. The Holy Spirit made contact early on and even took up residence within. However, my lack of knowledge regarding dual communication, righteousness in Him, and a real relationship that would enable truth in my life hindered God's healing work.

I needed the active reality of the Holy Spirit's Presence in my life so that Divine wisdom and revelation could enter in and bring the healing God desired for me. I needed the Holy Spirit Teacher to reveal His truth to me that would bring freedom.

The Holy Spirit reveals God's true nature

The Holy Spirit Teacher brings to light promises that are for us. Jeremiah 29:11 speaks of God's intention for our lives, " 'For I know the plans I have for you,' declares the LORD, 'plans to prosper you and not to harm you, plans to give you hope and a future.' "

God is all powerful, and His promises are far above all else. Psalm 33:6–7 (NLT) says, "The LORD merely spoke, and the heavens were created. He breathed the word, and all the stars were born. He assigned the sea its boundaries and locked the oceans in vast reservoirs."

That Scripture reminds me of the song "Redeemer." Nicole C. Mullen sings, "Who *taught* the sun where to stand in the morning? And who *taught* the ocean you can only come this far? And who *showed* the moon where to hide till evening?"[2]

When I initially remembered the song, before looking up the lyrics, I thought the words were significantly different. I replaced the words "taught" and "showed" with the word "told." It turns out I believed a lie that God was that kind of a teacher. A wrong belief system about God's true nature was being revealed to me, little by little.

Its unveiling came as I spent time with the Holy Spirit, who opened my eyes to what God was really like. One of the first things God showed me as I journeyed through healing was that He's not controlling.

Our Father is a good Teacher; He's not a dictator. He wants us to choose to sit in His classroom, relate with Him, and learn from Him. He wants to teach and show us how to live—not just tell us what to do or not to do.

In my high school days, I remember how the sight of a television rolling in on a metal cart brought immediate exuberance into the classroom. It was only second to the elation experienced when a new face sat at the desk, typically occupied by our regular teacher.

A substitute teacher was a reprieve from the monotony—a lift from the humdrum of the day. That's what having the Holy Spirit as our Teacher is like! He's not a regular teacher—He's Divine! His instructions always guide us toward health and wholeness. Dare I say, He's even fun?

Our Professor, the Holy Spirit, holds in His Presence the ability to bring renewal and refreshing to every part of our soul and body. A single Heavenly kiss full of healing power in my direction could wipe out any sign of sickness in an instant. Yet, my healing was a journey.

Hebrews 6:11–12 says, "We want each of you to show this same diligence to the very end, so that what you hope for may be fully realized. We do not want you to become lazy, but to imitate those who through faith *and* patience inherit what has been promised."

I didn't learn to believe things that weren't true about myself, others, and even about God overnight. My belief systems, tainted by life's experiences, needed truth and renewal if my health was going to improve—and it was going to take some time.

Deeper issues were going on beneath the illness. There were roots that God was willing to speak to me about. He was interested in tending to every wound and revealing the truth my soul needed to hear. A healthy body came as a result.

If only I had known I was being called to inquire of Him, to listen to the Teacher, and to see God for who He really was. I had faith and even patience, but I lacked the active direction and Presence of the only Person who could put fuel to the fire of His Word, to bring the healing He promised and wanted for me.

Answers through Holy Spirit relationship

What I was doing with food was a clue into the heartache God wanted to heal—if only I would turn to the Holy Spirit and listen for His truth. Nothing else could permanently satisfy the true longings of my soul.

My solution was as simple as going to the Father and allowing Him into every part of my soul. I began inviting Him to show me what I didn't yet know, to heal my hurts, and to allow His truth to replace the lies I was believing—about myself, Him, and others.

Walking in God's truth and relishing in His peace over my past and present circumstances were my reward. His peace became mine. It can be the same for you.

God taught me how to deal with my pain and unresolved emotions; He taught me how to come to Him for healing by receiving His truth. I'll share those principles with you next.

Heart Connection

1. Read the lyrics to "You Say" – Lauren Daigle.[3] I've provided a link for you here: https://www.azlyrics.com/lyrics/laurendaigle/yousay.html.

   Are any phrases resonating with you? If so, ask the Holy Spirit what He wants to communicate to you. In a journal, jot down what you hear.

2. Listen to the song "You Say."[4] I've provided a YouTube link for you here: https://www.youtube.com/watch?v=sIaT8Jl2zpI.

   What else is the Holy Spirit speaking to your heart? Be sure to write it down.

3. Are you able to distinguish your value apart from what you do or what other people think or say about you?

   Ask the Holy Spirit to reveal any area in your life where you are overly dependent on your accomplishments or the opinions of others.

4. Ask the Holy Spirit if there's an activity you consistently practice that causes you to avoid working through issues. Surrender it to God, ask Him to be your source of comfort, and invite Him to speak truth into your life.

5. Have you considered the Holy Spirit as your Teacher? Ask Him to reveal something to you. If you feel comfortable, share the truth you receive with someone else who may also benefit from it.

Chapter 17

Holy Spirit Soul Healing

Having the counsel of the Holy Spirit when we quiet ourselves to listen allows for the healing of our souls. This time of leaning close to the whispers of God often translates to physical healing as well—it did for me.

Healing your emotions that are connected to false messaging received from past experiences plays a major role in walking in wholeness. Your soul encompasses your mind, will, and emotions. You will be as healthy in your body to the degree these areas are prospering (3 John 1:2).

We are three-part beings and experience life through our spirit, soul, and body. Each part is independent and yet affects the others. Emotions and feelings are in the realm of our soul and must be tended to. Just as our body requires food and water to survive, and our spirit needs a Savior to be brought to life, so our soul prospers as we acknowledge and provide for its needs through the guidance and counsel of the Holy Spirit.

God desires to heal our souls, and He uses our emotions to lead us into truth. The truths we receive from the Holy Spirit can bring permanent freedom to any issue in our lives—past, present, and future. Destructive behavior patterns become subject to truth, and with that comes freedom. John 8:36 says, "So if the Son sets you free, you will be free indeed."

The mindsets we've cultivated have kept us from living in true freedom—mainly, the freedom to be ourselves.

It's time for the real you to shine!

Authenticity and acknowledging our emotions

Our souls cry out to be seen and heard. Accepting what is truly going on inside of us is a call to authenticity. Buried under inaccurate belief systems is our true self. When we don't acknowledge our genuine feelings, they fester and end up causing us to live below the life that's available to us as children of God.

Our truth, expressed through emotions, tells us what we believe about ourselves and others in relation to us. They are revelatory signposts bringing to the forefront what's really going on within.

Our emotions beg to be heard so healing can come. Bringing them into view, for Holy Spirit examination, is vital for soul healing and outward functioning. Many of us are marinating in the destructive consequences of not dealing honestly with ourselves. Our emotions have been denied a voice. They've been trying to communicate our genuine needs, but many of us have not been listening.

Pastor and author Rick Warren says, "You are only as sick as your secrets."[1] I found that statement to be true in my own life. My sick body was trying to tell me something. It was time to stop denying that intense emotions existed within my soul—and to deal with them.

The Lord led me to passages in Scripture where Jesus expressed a full spectrum of emotions. He felt compassion, wept, and even displayed anger. It helped me realize it was okay for me to feel too.

As a child, I wasn't allowed to express anger or disagree with set expectations. Fear was my constant companion. That pattern continued in my life, and the bottling up of emotions eventually manifested in a sick soul and body.

Jesus' emotions were pure and untainted by sin. He certainly wasn't in need of soul healing. When examining our emotions and reactions, we can't always say the same; that doesn't mean what we're feeling is any less significant.

I needed to express to the Lord how I really felt about things. In doing so, He could bring healing to my soul. Psalm 147:3 says, "He heals the brokenhearted and binds up their wounds."

My secrets were wrapped up in things I believed that at one time served me—they kept me safe. Later in life, as I behaved under those same belief systems, they proved to have negative results. Not standing up for myself in one season gave me a level of protection and was necessary. However, living under the same mindset as an adult had serious consequences.

Stuffing my emotions was a problem. Therapist and author Karol K. Truman penned an entire book on the subject called *Feelings Buried Alive Never Die.*[2] The title alone paints a clear picture of the hole I'd dug for myself and unknowingly shoveled my feelings into.

Their cries echoed throughout my physical body in the form of illness until I saw them for what they were. They were there to help me—be me. As I dealt with my feelings, instead of denying them, I began to mature and heal.

Emotions are indicators and aren't to be ignored

Many of us have learned early in childhood that emotions fall into good and bad categories. We've been forced to judge them and, even worse, to deny them altogether. We may have even been told how we should feel.

"Oh, you're fine; there's no reason to cry."

A classic message is that anger is bad, and in expressing it, we're doing something wrong.

"Stop acting that way, and go to your room."

Jesus expressed righteous anger over what was occurring at God's temple and in witnessing God's people being taken advantage of (Matthew 21:12–13; Mark 11:15–18; John 2:13–22). It showed me there are times when anger is justified, and its display is even necessary.

There are certain situations when anger is misplaced and unwarranted. But what if we were to look at emotions as neutral and our examination of them, along with the Holy Spirit, as a way to better ourselves, our relationships, and to bring healing?

Our emotions are great indicators pointing to what we believe about ourselves and others. They allow us an opportunity to peer into the window of our soul and, with the help of the Holy Spirit, to decipher what mindsets we're living under that are no longer serving us.

Heightened emotions are often reactions to belief systems that need transforming. If we ignore them or shame ourselves over them, we miss out on the messages they have for us.

As we acknowledge our emotions and find the truth behind them, we can come to a place where we respond to situations rather than react to them uncontrollably.

Knowing when emotions need Holy Spirit healing

When we have an overly heightened emotional reaction in a situation, we would do well to question if an area in our soul needs healing. Our emotions need to be managed, but it's only possible once we recognize them and discover what they are trying to tell us.

Strong emotions can reveal what we believe. That discovery, renewed by God's truth and in receiving His comfort, brings healing to our emotions. The emotions themselves don't cause harm; when our feelings are being ignored and left unresolved is when our souls and physical bodies pay a price. Often, our relationships suffer too.

I was an expert at hiding my true feelings. Anger and grief were my big two. It felt wrong to acknowledge that I missed out on so much as a child of immigrant parents, including the freedom to play instead of work and falling under incredible responsibilities long before I should have. I carried grief in my heart over what I'd missed out on.

Lurking beneath the grief was a tremendous amount of anger and bitterness that hadn't been dealt with. Carrying unresolved anger, unforgiveness, resentment, bitterness, regret, grief, sorrow, shame, rejection, etc. puts undue stress on our soul and body.

Our pain and emotions must be processed in the arms of our loving God. We can choose to let go of negative experiences and the emotions attached to them, so they no longer affect our health.

The Holy Spirit is willing to set us free from wrong belief systems and heal our pain. I'd like to teach you a simple process of healing with the Holy Spirit. It will help clear out destructive mindsets and their accompanying emotions that may be causing turmoil within your soul and body.

I've outlined ten steps as a guide to prompt conversation with your Healer. The Holy Spirit is unique in His healing process with every person. Be sensitive to His leading. He is the Healer, not a formula.

Holy Spirit Soul Healing Guide:

1. Acknowledge. When you find yourself reacting to situations or people outside of the parameters of the fruit of the Spirit, don't ignore what's happening. Galatians 5:22–23a (NLT) says, "But the Holy Spirit produces this kind of fruit in our lives: love, joy, peace, patience, kindness, goodness, faithfulness, gentleness, and self-control."

Our soul is attempting to communicate with us when we aren't walking in the fruit of the Spirit—we need to listen.

2. Ask. Once you've noticed that your reactions are incongruent with the fruit of the Spirit, ask the Holy Spirit to reveal why you're experiencing them. Remember, the Holy Spirit goes beyond human understanding and can take you directly to the source of your false mindsets and pain. He is the Revelator and will show you what you do not know.

He may bring you to the memory of an incident from long ago. He may speak to you about a current situation in your life needing His guidance. He may show you how you've shut your necessary voice of truth off—evidenced by your inability to set boundaries with others, etc.

3. Discover. As you talk to the Lord honestly about the defining moment you went through, you'll discover what He has to say about it. The Holy Spirit will reveal the truth about the situation. Your response to current situations in life have likely been shaped by what is being highlighted to you. If you're experiencing unrest over an existing situation, He will speak into it and bring His perspective.

You need to hear what the Holy Spirit has to say about your past and the present. Allow Him to show you any potential lies you believe about yourself or someone else.

It's important to recognize the situation you went through doesn't need to be something traumatic—although it can be. Sometimes, it's the small hurts or things we've brushed off that end up creating silent wounds in our souls and faulty belief systems. You may have been too young to know the impact they would carry and lacked the ability to process what happened at the time.

Seemingly insignificant things can affect us negatively years later. We may be responding to situations emotionally, without self-control, because our feelings have never had an opportunity to be expressed. We need a voice in the matter.

4. Feel and deal. Look at the situation the Holy Spirit has revealed to you and feel. Grieve your losses—cry, kick, scream, etc. Do whatever is necessary to get your emotions out. Be completely honest. You are free to feel!

Go through every emotion the situation caused you to feel and deal with any lies you believe and still react from today. There may be more than one emotion or mindset to deal with. You may begin with anger but then find that sadness remains. You may have believed you are not worthy, followed by the lie that people cannot be trusted, etc.

This activity is reserved for you and the Holy Spirit. It's not about the person who harmed you; it's about getting what's buried deep inside of you out in the open safely. In taking this step with the Holy Spirit, you will no longer harm yourself through denial and won't hurt anyone else in the process.

Talk to the Lord about the incident He brings to your remembrance, openly and honestly. I find journaling my feelings is helpful. Just remember, those writings are for your eyes only, and perhaps a therapist if you are working with one outside the counsel of the Holy Spirit.

There may be a time when the Holy Spirit leads you to confront a person or situation. For those of us who have had a difficult time standing up for ourselves, out of fear or false messaging from our past experiences, the Lord will bring you to a place of maturity in handling your current relationships.

Expressing your true feelings to someone in a way that is healing to a relationship instead of harmful is the benefit of having first resolved your pain with the Lord. You will come from a space of greater peace.

5. Healing. Release to God your hurts and every emotion associated with them. If you feel angry, give it to Him. If you feel sad, let Him take that from you too. If you feel ashamed, allow Him to cleanse you. Let Him love you! He will comfort you and give you the truth you need to heal.

You may find the Holy Spirit speaking kind Words over you with regard to a situation you've been in; perhaps He'll tell you what you should have heard at the time.

He may recreate the experience with Him in the memory, through a picture in your mind, and provide for you exactly what you should have been given by the people involved. They may have failed you, but God will provide what they couldn't as a result of their own woundedness.

Allow Him to fill in what was missing from your experience. He will bring wholeness to your soul as you communicate with Him amid your pain, and He doesn't stop there. He will give you a treasure in its place. He will give you something much better than you've currently been living under; He will give you the truth. That truth brings with it your freedom, transformation, and healing.

6. Exchange. Jesus is prophesied about in Isaiah 61:1–4, "The Spirit of the Sovereign Lord is on me, because the Lord has anointed me to proclaim good news to the poor. He has sent me to bind up the brokenhearted, to proclaim freedom for the captives and release from darkness for the prisoners, to proclaim the year of the LORD's favor and the day of vengeance of our God, to comfort all who mourn, and provide for those who grieve in Zion—to bestow on them a crown of beauty instead of ashes, the oil of joy instead of mourning, and a garment of praise instead of a spirit of despair. They will be called oaks of righteousness, a planting of the LORD for the display of his splendor. They will rebuild the ancient ruins and restore the places long devastated; they will renew the ruined cities that have been devastated for generations."

Every false mindset and emotion associated with the experience you're willing to surrender to God are now His. You can trade His peace for your worry, His joy for your mourning, acceptance instead of rejection, value rather than shame, confidence in place of fear, and hope for a bright future instead of regrets, etc. The lies you've believed, as a result of the actions perpetrated against you, and any faulty ways of thinking in your soul that have affected your emotional well-being are no longer yours. Jesus will take them all!

Isaiah 53:4–5 is another passage in Scripture that highlights how our Savior suffered in order to take upon Himself our sufferings, "Surely he took up our pain and bore our suffering, yet we considered him punished by God, stricken by him, and afflicted. But he was pierced for our transgressions, he was crushed for our iniquities; the punishment that brought us peace was on him, and by his wounds we are healed."

Jesus is willing to take every wound you've suffered, heal you, and give you something better. One of the biggest takeaways is the intimacy you will cultivate with Him as He takes you through the process. He comes not only to bring healing but also gives you something much more powerful in exchange—Himself!

7. Renounce the lies and declare the truth. The lies you once believed are no longer true about you. The truth is, they never were. Now it's time to make a conscious decision to no longer live under their deception.

This might look like saying, "I renounce the lie that I'm not worthy." Then, reinforce the truth, "I'm unique, and God loves me without conditions." Be sure to express what the Holy Spirit imparted to you. This isn't about your ability to self-affirm, that doesn't produce long-term results. You're speaking out the *Rhema* Words you received in your time with the Holy Spirit.

He may have spoken to you through a mental picture. Verbalize what you saw and take in the truth He gave you. Renewing your mind is part of the process. If a lie attempts to return, combat it with the truth you've received.

8. Forgive. Now that you've received healing through the love, compassion, and truth of Christ—it's your turn. Luke 6:37 says, "Do not judge, and you will not be judged. Do not condemn, and you will not be condemned. Forgive, and you will be forgiven."

You've received release from your sins through God's grace given to you as a free gift in Christ. You did nothing to earn it. The result of receiving freely is the ability to extend the same to others. Matthew 10:8b says, "Freely you have received; freely give."

The capacity to forgive others is a gift of grace God gives us. Philippians 2:13 (NLT) encourages us with this, "For God is working in you, giving you the desire and the power to do what pleases Him." Ask the Holy Spirit for His help if you're finding it difficult to forgive.

You may have never felt like forgiving the individuals who harmed you before this point because of the deep-seated emotions that were never expressed. Now that you've walked through healing with the Holy Spirit, you will be better able to offer forgiveness.

Being honest with your feelings and having grieved your losses puts you in a place of truth within yourself. With the knowledge that an exchange is available for something much better and the humble recognition that you, too, have harmed others and desire the same mercy be given to you—you will feel more willing and able to let things go. The Holy Spirit will help you.

Unforgiveness, bitterness, and resentment only entrap you. They must be cleared out of your soul for deep healing to take place. This isn't always easy, but the Holy Spirit will empower you to do it.

Also, recognize that one of the most important people you may need to forgive is yourself!

9. Ask for forgiveness. As a result of the wounds you've experienced, you may have reacted to people in ways that caused them harm. If so, ask God to forgive you.

Rest assured, with any act of repentance we're guaranteed this promise, "If we confess our sins, he is faithful and just and will forgive us our sins and purify us from all unrighteousness" (1 John 1:9).

He will show you if there's someone in your life you may need to ask forgiveness from. James 5:16a instructs, "Therefore confess your sins to each other and pray for each other so that you may be healed." Follow the leading of the Holy Spirit and His timing.

10. Saturate in truth. You've come away with a lot of truth from the Holy Spirit. Meditate on those truths. Romans 12:2a instructs, "Do not conform to the pattern of this world, but be transformed by the renewing of your mind." Wash in the truth of your righteousness in Christ, in who God is for you as a good Father, and in the Holy Spirit's continual power and Presence in your life to bring truth and healing.

Fulfilling your Kingdom purpose

Your journey with the Holy Spirit Healer will bring more than restoration to your body and greater intimacy with God. It produces further reward as you walk in the fullness of what God created you for.

Your healthy body is the vehicle you need to do what He has purposed for you. A sick soul drains you of energy that is waiting to be used for better purposes. In receiving prosperity of soul through the help of the Holy Spirit, your body will be strong to fulfill your calling. 3 John 1:2 (ESV) says, "Beloved, I pray that all may go well with you and that *you may be in good health, as it goes well with your soul.*"

The connection between the healing of your body and the health of your spirit and soul is undeniable. I'm living proof! My prayer is that you will partner with the Holy Spirit to help you heal too. Your destiny depends on it.

If we don't feel well in our bodies, we likely won't be able to fulfill the dreams God places in our hearts. God wants us to be healthy and for us to feel well so we can be full of joy and participate in the Kingdom work He has for us.

John 10:10b (AMPC; first italics in the original) says, "I came that they may have *and* enjoy life, and have it in abundance (to the full, *till it overflows*)." Jesus came because He cares about our level of joy and its overflow onto others. He is glorified through it.

God knows the delight it brings us to walk in the fullness of what He's created us for. That joy culminates as we see the effect it has on the people around us. God wastes nothing, and your own healing journey can be used to bless the life of another and help bring healing to them.

There is a glorious inheritance we have in one another as believers; according to Ephesians 1:18–19a, "I pray that the eyes of your heart may be enlightened in order that you may know the hope to which he has called you, *the riches of his glorious inheritance in his holy people*, and his incomparably great power for us who believe."

There is no greater fulfillment in life than to use what you've learned to help bring wholeness to another person. God restores your spirit, soul, and body and brings recompense as you walk in the joy, purpose, and fullness of all Jesus came to earth to give you. May it be yours through the power of the Holy Spirit in your life to heal.

"May the grace of the Lord Jesus Christ, and the love of God, and the fellowship of the Holy Spirit be with you all"
(2 Corinthians 13:14).

Heart Connection

1. Read the lyrics to "In the Garden" – Alan Jackson.[3] I've provided a link for you here: https://www.azlyrics.com/lyrics/alanjackson/inthegarden.html.

   Are any phrases resonating with you? If so, ask the Holy Spirit what He wants to communicate to you. In a journal, jot down what you hear.

2. Listen to the song "In the Garden."[4] I've provided a YouTube link for you here: https://www.youtube.com/watch?v=s1691J96_xc.

   What else is the Holy Spirit speaking to your heart? Be sure to write it down.

3. Do you find yourself being authentic with yourself by acknowledging your emotions?

   Ask the Holy Spirit if you're being true to yourself and in your relationships. Are you able to express your desires freely without fear? If not, ask the Holy Spirit to reveal the reason behind your inability to express yourself.

4. In implementing the steps to Holy Spirit Soul Healing, has God revealed some faulty belief systems you've been living under? What truth did He reveal to you? Write them down and meditate on them. Thank Him for restoring your soul with His truth.

5. Have you grieved the losses in your life? Allow the Holy Spirit to comfort you as you give Him what you feel you missed out on.

   Ask the Holy Spirit what exchange He's offering you in releasing the losses to Him. Rejoice over the restoration of your soul as you let go of the past and look to God for the good future He has for you. The fulfillment of your Kingdom purpose may very well be part of the reward!

   Read Jeremiah 29:11, " 'For I know the plans I have for you,' declares the LORD, 'plans to prosper you and not to harm you, plans to give you hope and a future.' "

Notes

Introduction: Are There Challenges You Think You Can't Overcome?

1. Hayes Mark and Carpenter Kelly, "Michael W. Smith Lyrics," AZLyrics, accessed November 15, 2020, https://www.azlyrics.com/lyrics/michaelwsmith/drawmeclose.html.

2. Worship Videos. "Michael W. Smith - Draw Me Close [with lyrics]," YouTube, February 23, 2012, video, https://www.youtube.com/watch?v=7d_0Yr-P16M&feature=youtu.be.

Chapter 1: The Lupus Octopus

1. Tracey Williams Strudwick, "What is a malar rash?," Medical News Today, last modified April 24, 2018, https://www.medicalnewstoday.com/articles/321594.

2. Mayo Clinic Staff, "Hypothyroidism (underactive thyroid)," Mayo Clinic, last modified November 19, 2020, https://www.mayoclinic.org/diseases-conditions/hypothyroidism/symptoms-causes/syc-20350284.

3. "Antinuclear Antibody Test," *Web*MD, last modified September 21, 2020, https://www.webmd.com/a-to-z-guides/what-is-an-antinuclear-antibody-test#1.

4. "ANA Testing," Lupus Research Alliance, accessed February 27, 2020, https://www.lupusresearch.org/understanding-lupus/diagnosis-and-treatment/ana-testing/.

5. "What doctors look for to confirm a diagnosis," Lupus Foundation of America, last modified July 25, 2013, https://www.lupus.org/resources/what-doctors-look-for-to-confirm-a-diagnosis.

6. David Thomas, "Octopuses have two legs and six arms," The Telegraph, last modified August 12, 2008, https://www.telegraph.co.uk/news/newstopics/howaboutthat/2547597/Octopuses-have-two-legs-and-six-arms.html.

7. "Octopus Physical Characteristics," OCTOPUSWORLDS, accessed November 16, 2020, https://octopusworlds.com/octopus-anatomy/.

8. "The history of lupus," Lupus Foundation of America, accessed February 27, 2020, https://www.lupus.org/resources/the-history-of-lupus.

9. Alana B. Levine, MD, "How Lupus Affects Multiple Organs," HSS, last modified December 17, 2015, https://www.hss.edu/conditions_many-faces-lupus-organ-involvement-SLE.asp.

10. Ibid.

11. Ibid.

12. Reuters Staff, "Octopuses have six 'arms' and two 'legs': study," Reuters, last modified August 14, 2008, https://www.reuters.com/article/us-octopus-research-idUSLE12120720080814.

13. "Lupus and Pregnancy," March of Dimes, last modified December, 2013,https://www.marchofdimes.org/complications/lupus-and-pregnancy.aspx.

14. Mason Babbie Y, "Jesus The One And Only." Musixmatch, accessed November 17, 2020, https://www.musixmatch.com/lyrics/Brooklyn-Tabernacle-Choir/Jesus-The-One-And-Only.

15. Bekkil5, "Jesus the One and Only - Brooklyn Tabernacle Choir," YouTube, February 14, 2012, video, https://youtu.be/oCSVNSi-UzY.

Chapter 2: Pain from the Past

1. "Mark Twain Quotes," Inspiration Station, accessed November 18, 2020, http://www.inspirationstation.info/mark-twain/mark-twain-quotes.html.

2. Victor Manuel Navejar and Travis Montorius Greene, "Travis Greene Lyrics," AZLyrics, accessed November 18, 2020, https://www.azlyrics.com/lyrics/travisgreene/intentional.html.

3. Travis Greene, "Travis Greene – Intentional (Official Music Video)," YouTube, October 15, 2015, video, https://www.youtube.com/watch?v=VH3f0ellNv8.

Chapter 3: The Psych Ward

1. Shawna De La Rosa, "Prednisone: The Steroid That Can Make You Feel Crazy," MedShadow, last modified May 30, 2019, https://medshadow.org/prednisone-psychiatric-side-effects/.

2. Andrew Holt, Mia Leanne Cherie Fieldes, and Hope Rachelle Darst, "The Belonging Co Lyrics," AZLyrics, accessed November 19, 2020, https://www.azlyrics.com/lyrics/belongingco/peacebestill.html.

3. music meets heaven, "Peace Be Still (Lyrics) ~ The Belonging Co ft. Lauren Daigle," YouTube, June 2, 2018, video, https://www.youtube.com/watch?v=VBzg4B3_yS8&feature=youtu.be.

Chapter 4: Kidney Disease & Chemotherapy

1. "Rise Up (Lazarus) Lyrics," ZionLyrics, accessed December 14, 2020, https://zionlyrics.com/cain-rise-up-lazarus-lyrics.

2. CAIN, "CAIN - Rise Up (Lazarus) [Official Lyric Video]," YouTube, March 6, 2020, video, https://www.youtube.com/watch?v=pw8Ig-PHRBr4&feature=youtu.be.

Chapter 5: Kidney Failure & Dialysis

1. "What Happens When Your Kidneys Fail?," New Health Advisor, last modified February 11, 2021, https://m.newhealthadvisor.org/What-happens-when-your-kidneys-fail.html.

2. Elisabeth Almekinder, "Diabetes And Renal Failure: Everything You Need To Know," TheDiabetesCouncil, last modified June 4, 2020, https://www.thediabetescouncil.com/diabetes-and-renal-failure-everything-you-need-to-know/.

3. "Dialysis," Wikipedia, last modified November 29, 2020, https://en.wikipedia.org/wiki/Dialysis.

4. "A Brief History of Dialysis," Dialysis Patient Citizens Education Center, last modified March 10, 2016, https://www.dpcedcenter.org/news-events/news/a-brief-history-of-dialysis/.

5. "Peritoneal dialysis," Wikipedia, last modified December 22, 2020, https://en.wikipedia.org/wiki/Peritoneal_dialysis.

6. "The Bathtub Presternal PD Catheter," Home Dialysis Central, accessed March 27, 2020, https://www.homedialysis.org/life-at-home/articles/the-bathtub-presternal-pd-catheter.

7. "What Is a Peritoneal Dialysis Machine," Fresenius Kidney Care, accessed March 27, 2020, https://www.freseniuskidneycare.com/ckd-treatment/what-is-dialysis/peritoneal-dialysis-machine.

8. "Kidney Failure: Loss of Appetite on Dialysis," Kidney Disease, accessed March 27, 2020, http://www.renaldiseases.org/kidney-failure-symptoms/704.html.

9. Walead Latif, "Diet - chronic kidney disease," MedlinePlus, last modified July 16, 2019, https://medlineplus.gov/ency/article/002442.htm.

10. Mathea Ford, "Foods To Avoid When You're on Dialysis," Renal Diet HQ, accessed March 29, 2020, https://www.renaldiethq.com/foods-avoid-youre-dialysis/.

11. "Signs of Potassium Deficiency: Do You Need More Potassium in Your Diet?," Health Guide Info, last modified February 26, 2009, https://www.healthguideinfo.com/nutrition-basics/p27506/.

12. Lisa Fayed, "What Is Hyperkalemia?," verywellhealth, last modified January 27, 2020, https://www.verywellhealth.com/hyperkalemia-overview-513927.

13. See note 10 above.

14. "Sodium and Chronic Kidney Disease," Davita Kidney Care, accessed March 29, 2020, https://www.davita.com/diet-nutrition/articles/basics/sodium-and-chronic-kidney-disease.

15. "Do You Know Where Salt Is Hiding in Your Food?," Cleveland Clinic, last modified September 14, 2020 https://health.clevelandclinic.org/know-salt-hiding-food/.

16. Janet Helm, "The Hidden Sodium in Chicken," CookingLight, last modified January 14, 2011, https://www.cookinglight.com/eating-smart/nutrition-101/sodium-in-chicken.

17. Joel Timothy Houston, Matthew Philip Crocker, and Salomon Ligthelm, "Hillsong United Lyrics," AZLyrics, accessed November 23, 2020, https://www.azlyrics.com/lyrics/hillsongunited/oceanswherefeetmayfail.html.

18. Hillsong UNITED, "Oceans (Where Feet May Fail) Lyric Video - Hillsong UNITED," YouTube, February 22, 2013, video, https://youtu.be/dy9nwe9_xzw.

Chapter 6: A Plea for Life Answered

1. "The Kidney Transplant Waitlist - What You Need to Know," National Kidney Foundation, last modified February 10, 2017, https://www.kidney.org/atoz/content/transplant-waitlist.

2. "Testing Involved in the Living Donor Evaluation Process," National Kidney Foundation, accessed March 29, 2020, https://www.kidney.org/transplantation/livingdonors/testing-living-donor-evaluation-process.

3. "Risk of Surgery," National Kidney Foundation, accessed March, 29, 2020, https://www.kidney.org/transplantation/livingdonors/risks-of-surgery.

4. Matthew Hein, Matthew Armstrong, Ethan Hulse, and Jon Mcconnell, "I AM THEY Lyrics," AZLyrics, accessed October 25, 2020, https://www.azlyrics.com/lyrics/iamthey/scars.html.

5. I AM THEY, "I AM THEY - Scars (Official Music Video)," YouTube. January 25, 2019, video, https://youtu.be/OqjGT9BSyJA.

Chapter 7: Opening Communication with God

1. "Line of communication," Wikipedia, January 16, 2020, https://en.wikipedia.org/wiki/Line_of_communication.

2. "When and why was the blood sacrifice required by God?," NeverThirsty, accessed April 25, 2020, https://www.neverthirsty. org/bible-qa/qa-archives/question/when-and-why-was-the-blood-sacrifice-required-by-god/.

3. Ben Fielding and Reuben Morgan, "Jeremy Camp Lyrics," AZLyrics, accessed October 25, 2020, https://www.azlyrics.com/lyrics/ jeremycamp/mightytosave.html.

4. JeremyCampMusic, "Jeremy Camp "Mighty To Save," YouTube, August 24, 2010, video, https://youtu.be/YVeQoHdIDEE.

Chapter 8: A Journey to Wholeness

1. Jules Yap, "IKEA 'Bully a Plant' experiment shows eye opening results," IKEAhackers, May 8, 2018, https://www.ikeahackers. net/2018/05/ikea-bully-a-plant-experiment.html.

2. Torwalt Bryan James and Torwalt Katie, "Francesca Battistelli Lyrics," AZLyrics, accessed November 28, 2020, https://www. azlyrics.com/lyrics/francescabattistelli/holyspirit.html.

3. FrancescaBattistelli, "Francesca Battistelli – Holy Spirit (Official Audio)," YouTube, April 22, 2014, video, https://youtu.be/UvBBC7-PSHo.

Chapter 9: The Holy Spirit for You & Me

1. Sarladue, "Welcome Holy Spirit," LyricsTranslate, last modified May 10, 2013, https://lyricstranslate.com/en/mark-condon-welcome-holy-spirit-lyrics.html.

2. Ibid.

3. Nikkyttlyricsworship, "Welcome Holy Spirit - Lyrics," YouTube, October 12, 2013, video, https://youtu.be/ch-b1VkttqQ.

Chapter 10: A Spiritual Language for Love & Power

1. Jude Del Hierro, "Michael W. Smith Lyrics," AZLyrics, accessed December 1, 2020, https://www.azlyrics.com/lyrics/michaelwsmith/morelovemorepower.html.

2. Cliftongs, "Michael W. Smith-More Love, More Power," YouTube, October 1, 2009, video, https://youtu.be/MhnmLNfyqY4.

Chapter 11: Your Righteous Identity

1. "What does the Bible say about Christian saints? What are saints?," compellingtruth, accessed January 24, 2020, https://www.compellingtruth.org/Christian-saints.html.

2. "Definition of God's Grace," All About God, accessed April 24, 2020, https://www.allaboutgod.com/definition-of-gods-grace-faq.htm.

3. Matthew G. Maher et al., "Matt Maher Lyrics," AZLyrics, accessed October 25, 2020, https://www.azlyrics.com/lyrics/mattmaher/lordineedyou.html.

4. Mattmahermusic, "Matt Maher - Lord, I Need You (Official Lyric Video)," YouTube, May 1, 2013, video, https://youtu.be/LuvfMDhTyMA.

Chapter 12: Our Father

1. Glory City Church, "Jesus Is The Truth About God | Mark Greenwood," YouTube, June 30, 2019, video, https://www.youtube.com/watch?v=SzL_aFA_vKk&feature=youtu.be.

2. Arlene R. Taylor, "Amount of Laughter," Realizations Inc., accessed April 29, 2020, https://arlenetaylor.org/laughter-humor-and-the-brain/4192-amount-of-laughter.

3. "Matthew 18:22," Bible Hub, accessed December 6, 2020, https://biblehub.com/commentaries/matthew/18-22.htm.

4. Mathew Foster et al., "Chris Tomlin Lyrics," AZLyrics, accessed December 6, 2020, https://www.azlyrics.com/lyrics/christomlin/goodgoodfather.html.

5. ChrisTomlinVevo, "Chris Tomlin - Good Good Father (Lyrics And Chords)," YouTube, October 14, 2015, video, https://www.youtube.com/watch?v=iBmwwwiHrOk.

Chapter 13: Intimacy with Our Healing God

1. "What does it mean that God is Jehovah-Rapha." CompellingTruth, accessed April 21, 2020, https://www.compellingtruth.org/Jehovah-Rapha.html.

2. "189. Akoé," Bible Hub, accessed April 21, 2020, https://biblehub.com/greek/189.htm.

3. Corinne O'Keefe Osborn, "Tinnitus Remedies," healthline, last modified August 8, 2019, https://www.healthline.com/health/tinnitus-remedies.

4. "Mustard seed," Wikipedia, last modified December 20, 2020, https://en.wikipedia.org/wiki/Mustard_seed.

5. Herbert M. Wolf, "Immanuel," Bible Study Tools, accessed December 5, 2020, https://www.biblestudytools.com/dictionary/immanuel/.

6. "Be Sure To Go To Sword Practice," Renner, accessed April 18, 2020, https://renner.org/article/be-sure-to-go-to-sword-practice.

7. "4487. rhéma," Bible Hub, accessed April 17, 2020, https://biblehub.com/greek/4487.htm.

8. Mark Virkler, "The Real Difference Between Logos and Rhema Words," Charisma, accessed April 17, 2020, https://www.charismamag.com/spirit/bible-study/38866-the-real-difference-between-logos-and-rhema-words.

9. "Jon Thurlow - Jesus, You're Beautiful Lyrics," SongLyrics, accessed October 25, 2020, http://www.songlyrics.com/jon-thurlow/jesus-you-re-beautiful-lyrics/.

10. Forerunner Music. "Jon Thurlow - Jesus You're Beautiful (Lyric Video) | Forerunner Music," YouTube, April 14, 2016, video, https://youtu.be/_FdaESoZKvg.

Chapter 14: Hearing from the Healer

1. "Monologue," Merriam-Webster.com Dictionary, accessed May 4, 2020, https://www.merriam-webster.com/dictionary/monologue.

2. "We Have Two Ears, One Mouth (And Many More Ascriptions...)," Sententiae Antiquae, last modified January 30, 2020, https://sententiaeantiquae.com/2020/01/30/we-have-two-ears-one-mouth-and-many-more-ascriptions/.

3. "Eugene O'Neill," Wikipedia, accessed May 3, 2020, https://en.wikipedia.org/wiki/Eugene_O%27Neill; see note 2 above.

4. John J. Parsons, "Torah of Surrender...," Hebrew for Christians, accessed May 4, 2020, https://www.hebrew4christians.com/Meditations/Be_Still/be_still.html.

5. Christopher Cleveland, Casey Brown, and Parker Welling, "Stars Go Dim Lyrics," AZLyrics, accessed December 7, 2020, https://www.azlyrics.com/lyrics/starsgodim/youknowmebetter.html.

6. Stars Go Dim, "Stars Go Dim - You Know Me Better (Official Lyric Video)," YouTube, August 29, 2018, https://youtu.be/pOGlS5yz3zs.

Chapter 15: Revelation through a Dream

1. "33 Bible Verses about Rainbow," Knowing Jesus, accessed December 9, 2020, https://bible.knowing-jesus.com/topics/Rainbow.

2. Josh Thomas Bronleewe, Benji Coward, and Chris McClarney, Chris McClarney Lyrics," AZLyrics, accessed December 11, 2020,https://www.azlyrics.com/lyrics/chrismcclarney/imlistening.html.

3. Jesus Culture, "Chris McClarney - I'm Listening (Ft. Hollyn) (Official Audio)," YouTube, June 14, 2018, video, https://www.youtube.com/watch?v=nT8iKdwbKdU.

Chapter 16: Freedom in Truth

1. Joyce Meyer Ministries, "Recognize Your Who and Do in Christ | Joyce Meyer," YouTube, November 14, 2020, video, https://youtu.be/q9eeWEBKmv4.

2. Nicole Coleman Mullen, "Nicole C. Mullen Lyrics," AZLyrics, accessed November 18, 2020, https://www.azlyrics.com/lyrics/nicolecmullen/redeemer.html.

3. Jason Ingram, Paul Brendon Mabury, and Lauren Daigle, "Lauren Daigle Lyrics," AZLyrics, accessed December 17, 2020, https://www.azlyrics.com/lyrics/laurendaigle/yousay.html.

4. Lauren Daigle, "Lauren Daigle - You Say (Official Music Video)," YouTube, July 13, 2018, video, https://www.youtube.com/watch?v=sIaT8Jl2zpI.

Chapter 17: Holy Spirit Soul Healing

1. Rick Warren, "Quotable Quote," Goodreads, Inc., accessed October 26, 2020, https://www.goodreads.com/quotes/670756-you-re-only-as-sick-as-your-secrets.

2. Karol K. Truman, "Karol K. Truman," Goodreads, Inc., accessed October 27, 2020, https://www.goodreads.com/author/show/1560.Karol_K_Truman.

3. C. Austin Miles and Robert Hebble, "Alan Jackson Lyrics," AZLyrics, accessed October 29, 2020, https://www.azlyrics.com/lyrics/alanjackson/inthegarden.html.

4. Alan Jackson, "In The Garden," YouTube, April 18, 2015, video, https://www.youtube.com/watch?v=s1691J96_xc.

Acknowledgments

This book is the direct result of a gracious God who gives all things necessary in completing the work He's begun. He is the Author and the Finisher, and I'm in awe of His goodness in providing those who were willing to help see me through this labor of love.

The following is a list of those who held up my arms when I couldn't or didn't know how:

To my husband, Ben, thank you for your endless encouragement, continual prayers, and steadfast love. You are my gift of God's grace.

To Nathan—my *why*. I love you more than words can say.

To Leif, Vikki, & Carli Skulborstad, you've blessed my heart and life with more than I thought was possible. Thank you for showing me love in its purest form.

To the army God sent for me, Leigh Abbott and Michelle Morgan— thank you for helping me to heal. Your love is tangible.

To my prayer shield, thank you for standing with me. Sarah Hoving, Vikki Skulborstad, Sherri Lempe, Kitty Uhle, Betsy Clarke, Shelly Busby, and Jenny Carlson. You fought spiritual battles with prayers from your heart to His. I'm, on my knees, grateful!

Jendayi Harris, you're a person of God-strength, excellence, and dedication. Thank you for inspiring me to see the birth of this book through. Your prayers and encouragement were powerful, every time.

To my editor Amy Colvin, I'm incredibly grateful for your patience and generosity in answering all my questions—thank you for your time and essential contribution! To my proofreader Michael Jarnebro, your attention to detail put my mind at ease and I'm thrilled I found you. Sharon Roman, you're a brilliant friend with many talents, including wondrous grammar skills—thank you for always being available to help, I appreciate you! Linda Wilson, thank you for swooping in just in time with your willingness to help and for your valuable advice!

Thanks to Zonya Hamilton (Photoz by Zonya) for interior and exterior author photos. You're a skilled photographer and master of perfect settings and lighting! Daliborka Mijailovic, you created a gorgeous cover design and I'm grateful for your talent and patience with me throughout the process. Thank you to Joris Sharpe with Cutting Edge Studio for helping with the production of this book, but mostly for caring, all the way from the Netherlands. Lara Wille-Swink, I'm grateful for your faithful friendship over the years. Thank you for your help with the final polishing touches to the manuscript. You made it shine!

To my best friends in life, the ones who hear the real me and love me still. Your friendship means the world to me. Josh McKenna (Joshy), I wouldn't want to do life without you. Stephanie Whitrock, you're the sister I always wanted and now have. Brooke Severyn, you're a friend turned family. Sherri Lempe, even distance can't damper our David and Jonathan bond. Heather Dugan, thank you for wonderful conversations where inevitably we tap into Holy Spirit Truth—helping us to see more clearly. I'll never forget your help at the eleventh hour and am humbled by your selfless kindness and support.

To all my clients, I'm proud of you. I salute you and care for you deeply.

For those named and unnamed who have offered prayers, friendship, and encouragement throughout this journey—thank you for blessing me and for participating in God's Kingdom work. May you be blessed and God glorified!

What's Next?

- If you haven't received your free bonus chapter, "Beauty for Ashes: Even if You Start the Fire," do it now! Contact me at www.mimikrogerauthor.com to receive your copy, and stay tuned for emails with more wellness content coming your way!

- Check out my photo gallery for pictures related to *Holy Spirit, Help Me Heal* at mimikrogerauthor.com/photogallery.

- I would love to hear from you! Please share your testimony with me at www.mimikrogerauthor.com.

- Please send speaking invitations for your next event, conference, or podcast to mimikrogerauthor@gmail.com.

- Do you know someone who would benefit from reading *Holy Spirit, Help Me Heal*? Share the love with a friend by purchasing a copy for them, or direct them to my website: www.mimikrogerauthor.com for information on how to order.

- Explore my recommended reading and listening list.

- Please consider making a tax-deductible donation to 3 John 2 Ministries, a non-profit organization equipping individuals on how to connect with the Holy Spirit, nourish their souls through that connection and heal their physical body as a result. For more information visit: www.mimikrogerauthor.com/3john2ministries.

- Did *Holy Spirit, Help Me Heal* benefit you? Please leave a book review!

Recommended Reading & Listening List

- The #1 best-seller of all time: The Bible (any version)

- *Smith Wigglesworth Devotional* by Smith Wigglesworth

- *The Sacred Journey: God's Relentless Pursuit of Our Affection* by Brian & Candice Simmons

- *21 Ways to Finding Peace & Happiness: Overcoming Anxiety, Fear, and Discontentment Every Day* by Joyce Meyer

- *Emotional Healing in 3 Easy Steps* by Praying Medic

- *Who is the Holy Spirit?* Interview with David Diga Hernandez on *Sid Roth's It's Supernatural!* https://youtu.be/OAa15h4fk8s

- *Healing Scriptures* by John Hagee https://youtube/9qxfyyYDF58

Can You Help?

Please leave an Amazon review,
encouraging others toward their next step to wholeness!

If you purchased your book through another book retailer,
please leave your review on their site.

I appreciate your feedback, and would love to hear
what you have to say about your personal experience reading

Holy Spirit, Help Me Heal.

*Thank you for allowing me to be a part of your healing journey.
I'm grateful for you and pray God's richest blessings over
your spirit, soul, & body.*

With love,
Mimi

About the Author

Mimi Kroger began her life in Brooklyn, New York. The child of immigrant parents from Italy and Argentina, she lived the life of an American with old-world roots influencing her day-to-day life. At a young age, her family moved from New York to the beautiful mountains of Colorado. Her life took a dramatic turn in 1993 with a lupus diagnosis culminating in a kidney transplant 21 years later. Her relationship with Christ gave her the grace to fight, and as she became more intimately acquainted with the Holy Spirit, she began to heal. Health issues inspired her career as a group fitness instructor, nutrition guide, and personal trainer. Receiving healing has spurred on her calling further as an author, speaker, and behavior change specialist. She is compelled to bring life, health, and wholeness through what she has learned, both spiritually and professionally.

Website: mimikrogerauthor.com
Email: mimikrogerauthor@gmail.com

Author Photos by Zonya Hamilton,
Photoz by Zonya

HEALTH & FITNESS

Mimi and her husband, Ben Kroger, are the owners of Sozo Health and Fitness, a wellness company established in 2013. *Sozo* in Greek means to "Save, deliver, protect from, to heal, preserve, do well, or to be made whole."

Their mission is to ensure that every individual pursuing health and wellness be equipped with the knowledge and understanding needed to accomplish abundant life and wholeness.

They would like to help you! For all available Sozo Health and Fitness services, including personal training, online training, nutritional guidance, corporate wellness programs, gym set-up, and behaivor change coaching...

Check out their website:
www.sozohealthandfitness.com

73348120R00168